$4.95

FALSE GOD

HOW THE GLOBALIZATION MYTH
HAS IMPOVERISHED CANADA

JAMES LAXER

Lester Publishing Limited

Copyright © 1993 by James Laxer
All rights reserved. No part of this work covered by the copyrights hereon
may be reproduced or used in any form or by any means—graphic, electronic or
mechanical, including photocopying, recording, taping or information storage
and retrieval systems—without prior written permission of the publisher or,
in the case of photocopying or other reprographic copying, a licence from the
Canadian Reprography Collective. Lester Publishing Limited acknowledges the
financial assistance of the Canada Council and the Ontario Arts Council.

Canadian Cataloguing in Publication Data

Laxer, James, 1941-
      False god: how the globalization myth has
          impoverished Canada

ISBN 1-895555-09-4

1. Canada—Economic conditions—1991- .*
2. United States—Economic policy—1981-
I. Title.

HC115.L39   1993   330.971   C93-093462-8

Lester Publishing Limited
56 The Esplanade
Toronto, Ontario
Canada M5E 1A7

Printed and bound in Canada

93 94 95 96 5 4 3 2 1

As some form of political loyalty is part of the good life,

and as we are not flexible enough to kneel to the

rising sun, we must be allowed to lament the passing

of what had claimed our allegiance.

— GEORGE GRANT, *LAMENT FOR A NATION*

Give us twenty years ... and you will not

recognize this country.

— BRIAN MULRONEY, IN HIS FIRST SPEECH TO THE HOUSE OF

COMMONS AS PRIME MINISTER

To Liz, Cathy, and Daphne

CONTENTS

Introduction and Acknowledgements   vii

1. The Reality of the New Global Age   1

2. An Age of American Decline   39

3. A Canadian Choice   89

Notes   139

INTRODUCTION AND ACKNOWLEDGEMENTS

This year Canadians will vote in a federal election that will almost certainly have a determining effect on the fate of their country well into the twenty-first century. They will be deciding whether they want Canada to be sovereign and effective in a new global age, or are content to let their country bind itself ever more tightly to the United States. Consciously or not, Canadians will be passing judgment on something called "globalization."

"Globalization" is a shorthand term for the doctrines the Conservative government has supported since it was elected in September 1984. The Conservatives have transformed Canada by entering into the Free Trade Agreement with the United States and by agreeing to join an extended agreement that includes Mexico. They have discarded the traditional Canadian idea of an active role for government in economic development, while working assiduously to undermine Canadian social programs. In sum, they have adopted the Reagan–Bush economic and social model, blind to the vast problems that have motivated Americans themselves to reject this model.

The present government serves a god it calls "globalization."

A great conceit of the Conservatives and of the business lobbyists and "thinkers" who surround them is that they alone are in touch with the way the world is changing. Like old-fashioned schoolmasters, they see it as their duty to teach Canadians to mend their ways.

In one respect I agree with the Conservatives: the world *has* been changing—but not at all in the ways they claim it has. The sacrifices the Conservatives have demanded have been to placate a false god. Canadians have been sold a false analysis of the world and then been prodded into accepting changes in their society that have nothing to do with their well-being.

Conservatism, it turns out, is not about ever greater effectiveness; rather, it is about greed and social division. For Canadians the consequences of Conservative rule have been catastrophic. In the great recession of the early 1990s, no economy has been more severely battered than Canada's. Never has the Canadian state lacked legitimacy with the Canadian people the way it does today. Never has the very survival of the Canadian federation been more threatened.

In this book I am challenging the claim that the Conservatives are global realists. I am also presenting an alternative analysis of the new global age and a radically different perspective on how Canadians should adapt to it.

I have been motivated to write this book by the outrage I feel at the way that the Conservative government has presented a false picture of the world to Canadians. Those who have ruled this country for the past decade have sought to engender a mood of fatalism so that Canadians will simply accept what is being done to them and to their country.

I hope that this analysis of the realities of the new global age will counter the myths offered by those who have talked endlessly about "globalization" and also contribute to a more realistic and hopeful sense of what Canadians can achieve together.

A number of people helped me greatly in writing this book. The idea for it came from Malcolm Lester, and I am grateful to him for his constant support and encouragement as it was being planned and written. Gerald Caplan and Patricia Aldana commented on a draft of the manuscript and made invaluable suggestions for improvements. I am particularly grateful to Linda McQuaig, who read the manuscript at several stages, raising problems and asking pointed questions that forced me to clarify the issues with which this book deals. Matthew Kudelka did a first-class editing job. To my colleagues in the Political Science department at Atkinson College, York University—particularly Michael Henderson, David Davies, and Sten Kjellberg—I wish to express my gratitude for the personal support and collegiality they offered while this work was in progress. I am much indebted to my wife, Sandy Price, for encouraging me in writing this book and for making invaluable suggestions relating to the issues it covers.

CHAPTER ONE

THE REALITY OF THE NEW GLOBAL AGE

Prior to the election of the Progressive Conservatives in 1984, Canadians were nation builders. This was not a showy thing, directed at patriotic occasions. The focus was on making a living or, more broadly, on developing communities. In the process, Canadians were forging economic links with each other and with the outside world. From the start of European settlement, Canadian life always involved political, cultural, religious and, of course, economic connections with the outside world. But the emphasis was unmistakable: it was on the development of the country itself.

The Conservative government came to power determined to wrench Canadians out of this traditional nation-building mould. From the start, the government had a mission: to change the way Canadians thought about both their country and the world. The Conservatives meant to radically alter many of the central truths of Canadian life. For Brian Mulroney and his ministers the problem was clear—the world had become ruthlessly competitive; and the solution was simple—if Canadians hoped to survive in the tough new conditions that prevailed in the late twentieth century, they were going to have to give up much that had been familiar, and adopt instead a harsh, alien ethic that was more characteristic of the United States than of Canada.

To pressure Canadians to change their ways, the prime minister and his colleagues have relied on a single concept, indeed a single word—"globalization." Their highest priority has been to convince Canadians that this is the age of globalization and that its dictates must be followed. In preparing Canada for this Brave New World, their agenda has always been perfectly straightforward: to lead Canada into a comprehensive economic union with the United States that will require Canadians to adopt American approaches not only to the economy but also to society and politics. In Brian Mulroney, Canada has had a prime minister who believed in the American way of life and who was committed to bestowing its full blessings on his fellow citizens.

What gives the Conservative government its fateful importance is that it holds office at a critical juncture in the evolution of the global economy and in the structure of global power. The choices Canadians must now make are basic ones that will affect Canadian society and politics for decades to come.

The central argument of this book is that the Conservative government has carried out a wilful assault on Canada's institutions, traditions, and society. Further, this assault has been made in the name of globalization, which is a false god that has done vast destruction in many parts of the world. While Canadians did not invent globalization, they may well be the first people to preside over the dissolution of their country as a direct result of obeying its commandments.

The very survival of Canada has never been more in doubt than it is now. To a great degree, this is because the Conservative government has embraced the idea of globalization and all its consequences.

Canadian decision-makers have dangerously compartmentalized reality. Wearing one set of hats, they have been confronting the "Canadian question," trying to work out a durable constitutional solution for Canada. Wearing another set of hats, they have been grappling with the new global economy, the problems of the welfare state, and the limits to and possibilities for state action in the new global age. The result, as all Canadians know, has been the unravelling of Canada. During the disastrous referendum campaign on constitutional renewal in the autumn of 1992, Brian Mulroney desperately wanted to be seen affirming Canada. The tragedy is that his government stood for the systematic elimination of much about the Canadian experience that has been most worth keeping. Mulroney seemed to believe that Canada would still be intact if none of its provinces seceded, if it kept its membership in the G7, and if it became a free trade partner of the United States and Mexico. It has never occurred to him that if the idea of Canada is jettisoned, the country will lose its cohesiveness and may actually dissolve. With Canada now on the edge of disintegration, it is surely time to think critically about the ideas that have dominated us for the past decade and to consider the alternatives.

A New Global Age

We live in a new global age, although it does not at all resemble the new global age as set out by the school of thought to which the Conservative government ascribes.

In this new age, much that was long predictable has been rendered unpredictable. In May 1992 Mikhail Gorbachev met with Ronald Reagan at the former president's ranch in California. The two men, whose previous encounters had been at the pinnacle of their global power, were wearing cowboy hats. Not far away, Los Angeles had just been devastated by the worst American riots in a century. The state Gorbachev had led no longer existed; the nation whose reawakening Reagan had proclaimed was licking its wounds. The successor states of the Soviet Union were chaotic welfare cases, their governments counting on American know-how for salvation. For their part, Americans were increasingly unsure of their country's global position—a fact that accounted for the unusual turbulence of the presidential election campaign of 1992. In place of the "red scares" of the Cold War era, there was widespread anxiety concerning Japan. The days when Americans had been zealously looking for Moscow agents in the government and in Hollywood were ancient history. Now Americans were lining up to club Toyotas in the streets.

Old associations are dissolving, and new ones are forming. Any new age is bewildering, disconcerting, and exhilarating. We experience loss and excitement. There is no avoiding a new age: it will not go away, however much we might wish it would. Our responsibility is to face it, to comprehend it, and to preserve those basic values which need not change with the new circumstances.

The shock waves of the new historical era are being felt throughout the industrialized world. In many countries effective national sovereignty is declining. In extreme cases ethnic strife or even civil war is the result. Particularly in eastern Europe and the ex-Soviet Union, but elsewhere as well, ethnic consciousness is on the rise, accompanied in some places by the threat—and sometimes by the reality—of "ethnic cleansing." Yet at the same time, there is a growing movement towards the consolidation of enormous multistate economic blocs. The disorientation resulting from all of this is universal. At the level of our understanding of what constitutes a sovereign state and its role in society, the transformation we are now experiencing is the most profound one since the French Revolution.

Life is always made up of continuities and discontinuities. Even as our surroundings are changing, we can choose to focus on those things which remain the same—to shrink, if we like, from what is happening. From my home in Toronto, it is easy for me to think that things will go on much as they have in the past. My job will be in the same place. My relatives will live in the same Canadian cities. My relationship with my neighbours, my city, my province, and my country will go on much as in the past. As I write this, the Conservative government is telling me, in expensive, glossy television advertisements, that my citizenship is terribly important and that I should not take it for granted. In my suspicious way, I conclude that if the Conservative government, which never cared much for Canadian citizenship before, is now telling me how much it matters, then something dramatic must presently be happening to devalue it.

The Canada that was built by my grandfather's generation was conceived as a great new nation state—in effect, as a buffer between two global powers, Britain and the United States. As we grew in population, wealth, and mastery over our immense country, it was confidently expected that we would come of age. Our federal and provincial parliaments would make the critical decisions about political and social life in our country. Our votes would matter, in that they expressed our solidarity as citizens of a sovereign state. Such expectations were typical of people who lived in the Western, democratic world, where the idea of citizenship had been increasingly accepted ever since the Enlightenment and the French Revolution.

All of this now seems antique. We no longer trust our elected governments to make important decisions; in fact, we aren't even sure they have the capacity to make them. Instead, we have come to expect our governments to spend their time wrangling about their own impotence while circumstances they cannot control dictate policies to them. New technologies, global environmental changes, and recessions sweep in on us, and as they do, the federal government—the largest institution we have in common as Canadians—appears unable to act in any constructive way. Increasingly, for salvation, we are looking to multinational corporations and to a new collective leadership of the industrialized countries in which our own prime minister has little influence. Our citizenship has become something we dust off from time to time for nostalgic reasons; we no longer assume that it is a means to make ourselves heard when national decisions must be made.

The crisis that now threatens Canada arose from within. However, these internal stresses have been greatly heightened by new global forces that are now wrenching Canada into a new and unfamiliar shape. The new Canada is barely intelligible to our decision makers, who do not know how to deal with an altered world system that has greatly changed the way that Canadians relate to each other. British Columbians naturally focus on the rising power centre of East Asia; Quebeckers, who have remade their society in recent decades and established a new business class, are most concerned about winning new markets for themselves in Europe and the United States; Ontarians, long used to occupying the central place in Canadian life, are becoming increasingly anxious about how the technological revolution and the shifting global division of labour will affect their long-established—and vulnerable—manufacturing sector.

As the twentieth century draws to a close, Canadians find themselves facing a terrible dilemma. All nations are being drawn inexorably into the wider world; however, for Canadians, the pressures to conform to the new global order come primarily from the United States. And the United States, as we shall see, faces the very real prospect that it will be the first victim of the new global age. Our dilemma is this: how do we face the necessary challenges of the new age without becoming victims of the socio-economic crisis that now threatens the United States?

A key characteristic of the new global era is the proliferation of economic blocs, whose member countries make long-term and multifaceted economic arrangements among themselves. The existence of such blocs, wherever they are found, raises profoundly important issues relating to the prerogatives of elected governments. The blocs establish orderly commercial arrangements that transcend the borders of their member states; but they also vastly reduce the sovereignty of those states, and in doing so encroach on their internal democracy. In Europe the constraining of social, economic, and cultural policy to fit the narrow limits imposed by a larger economic bureaucracy has resulted in what critics refer to as a "democratic deficit." Debating and overcoming that deficit has become a top priority among member states of the European Community.

In our own case, the Canada–U.S. Free Trade Agreement, which went into effect on January 1, 1989, has diminished Canadian sovereignty. (Its successor, the North American Free Trade Agreement, which will bring Mexico into the bloc, will diminish it further.) The FTA does much more than establish a tariff-free regime between Canada and the United States; through it Canadians have traded away important powers to make domestic decisions. Ostensibly, we have gained assured access for our products to the American market; in fact, we have opened the door to almost wholly unregulated access for American investors in Canada. The FTA guarantees American firms the right of "national treatment" in Canada, while denying us the right to establish a two-price system for Canadian oil, under which we could pay lower prices than Americans for our own petroleum. (Such a regime existed for much of the 1970s and early 1980s.) It requires that we sustain our oil and natural gas exports to the United States during periods of petroleum shortage. It allows American firms to claim compensation from any Canadian government, federal or provincial, that decides to take a sector into public ownership. (American insurance companies warned the Ontario government in 1990 that they would expect compensation for their loss of market potential should the province set up a system of public auto insurance.)

In these and other ways, the FTA has set rules for Canada's economic and industrial policies. The FTA is a real, if unacknowledged, "fourth level of government," planted atop the municipal, provincial, and federal levels.

It is clear that Canada faces entirely new problems in addition to its perennial ones. It remains for me to show that these new problems are a direct result of the onset of a new global age.

THE GLOBALIZATION HYPOTHESIS

Over the past decade, especially in Britain and the United States, the apostles of "globalization" have dominated analysis of the state of the world. Those who present the globalization hypothesis have a particular method of analyzing how the world is changing and a set of prescriptions for how to deal with the economic crisis brought on by those changes.

While we are indeed living in a new global age, its character is not that claimed by the globalization "industry." To understand why this is so, it is important to realize that the globalization hypothesis is far from being a disinterested portrayal of our era. Indeed, it is more a product of the appetites of dominant business interests, than it is of the actual state of the world.

The concept of globalization has arisen at a very particular historical moment. In practical terms, it is the conventional wisdom of the English-speaking world's business élite in an era overshadowed by two great geopolitical events: the collapse of Soviet communism, and the rise of alternative forms of advanced capitalism in Japan and western Europe.

For their part, Canadians have been the recipients of an endless stream of offerings intended to convince them of the need to obey the dictates of globalization. Right at the beginning of the Mulroney era, there was the Report of the Royal Commission on the Economic Union and Development Prospects for Canada,[1] a commission chaired by Donald Macdonald, the former Liberal finance minister. The report has been used ever since as a justification for the Free Trade Agreement with the United States. Books and articles by economists such as Richard Lipsey, John Crispo, and Carl Beigie, reports for the C. D. Howe and Fraser Institutes, and policy positions taken by the Business Council on National Issues (BCNI) have advanced the same broad case. The editorial pages of the *Globe and Mail* and the *Financial Post* have restated the globalization hypothesis on a daily basis. And Canadians have seen the case boiled down for them in television commercials served up by the Government of Canada and paid for by the taxpayers.

The globalization hypothesis has enabled conservatives to look like revolutionaries who are in tune with the vast historical changes of our age. For well over a decade, conservatives have been making the case that revolutionary changes in technology, business practices, and the international division of labour are compelling society to adopt a tough and realistic approach to stiff competitive challenges from abroad. In the process, they have developed the body of thought we call globalization. While this world view can be depicted accurately as neoconservative, we shall soon see that it is far from being a partisan affair of the political parties of the right. As the dominant idea in the English-speaking world—and globalization is very much a product of Britain and the United States—it has influenced every political tendency. In the United States, most Democrats subscribe to it, as do the Liberal Democrats and many Labourites in Britain, and many Liberals and New Democrats in Canada.

The basic principles of globalization are familiar to almost everyone. Basically, they are these.

- We in the rich countries of the developed world are facing unprecedented competitive challenges as a consequence of the techno-revolution and the rise of Japan and the newly industrializing countries such as South Korea and Taiwan.
- Our society has grown so fat and lazy that we lack the economic will to meet the rigours of these challenges.
- We must and can shape up. This will involve slimming down, which in economic terms means cutting two types of costs: the cost of labour, and the cost of social and economic programs.
- While trimming those costs may be painful, society needs this bitter medicine. Once we have administered it to ourselves, we will all be rewarded by increased exports and higher living standards, and

we will have restored our ethical worth as well as
our capacity for self-reliance.

Cost cutting, of course, is not socially neutral; it establishes a very clear hierarchy of winners and losers and is based on precise notions about what is essential and what is secondary in contemporary society. According to the globalization hypothesis, the marketplace is at the centre of society and the most important people in it are the entrepreneurs, because they are the ones who take risks investing their money and managing large and small enterprises. It is they who carry the whole of society forward by responding creatively to the ever-shifting whims of the market. Military metaphors are often used to convey their valour, so that we are asked to picture them at the "front lines," "in the trenches," or engaged in "hand-to-hand combat." All other members of society should acknowledge their debt to this vital social phalanx, without whom any hope of prosperity would vanish. Globalization mythology continues that, because of their importance, businesspeople should be given all possible incentives to redouble their efforts. And while investors and managers are being encouraged by tax cuts and subsidies, the rest of society should not be entitled to higher wages and salaries, to better working conditions, or to improved social and environmental programs.

In the 1960s it was fashionable to celebrate the activities of those young people who donated their labour to projects of social and economic development, either at home or in the Third World. Now it is more in tune with the times to praise those energetic young lawyers who work around the clock and through their weekends with the goal of one day winning a partnership in a prestigious firm. This choice of social exemplars tells us much about how values change with the historical times.

The advocates of globalization have apparently given us a straightforward economic analysis and a set of policies that flow from that analysis. In actual fact, what we have is a doctrine that justifies social hierarchy and inequality. The true goal of globalization is not at all obscure: it is to reverse the movement towards greater social equality that occurred to varying degrees in every industrial country during the postwar decades. The rationale for reversing that tide is always the same: because of heightened competition, society can no longer afford social democracy, so expensive social and educational programs must be curtailed in order that we can resume healthy economic growth.

Those who support the tenets of globalization have typically presented themselves as apostles of change, to make it appear that, in our time, they alone have the courage to face up to the revolutionary social and economic developments taking place throughout the world.

When international Marxism disintegrated with the collapse of the Soviet Union, the hour of globalization had apparently arrived. Friedrich von Hayek and Milton Friedman can be seen as the Marx and Engels of market ideology, just as Margaret Thatcher and Ronald Reagan have been its Stalin and Mao. Freeing capital to operate globally required a powerful and coherent assault on the ideas and institutions that stood in the way. The nation-state and the idea of citizenship were the main barriers in the path of the globalization doctrine, and adherents of that doctrine led the assault against both. (Like Stalin and Mao, Thatcher and Reagan were far from perfect exemplars of the faith, in that they displayed xenophobia even while campaigning for the universal rights of capital.)

The market ideology that emerged in the English-speaking world during the 1970s and 1980s found a ready home on the political right, among American Republicans and British and Canadian Conservatives. However, we should not ignore that the new ideology was as much an expression of liberalism as it was of conservatism. Indeed, in continental Europe, the term "liberalism" was regularly applied to the Reagan–Thatcher brand of *laissez-faire* economics. When Jacques Chirac, a conservative, became the French prime minister in 1986, his tilt toward privatization and deregulation was always referred to as "liberalism." In Britain, traditional conservatives regularly dismissed Margaret Thatcher as a hard-edged Manchester school liberal who cared more about the market than conservative values. In the United States, neoconservatives were often dismissed by those further to the right; for example, during the Republican primaries in 1992, Patrick Buchanan worked hard to discredit George Bush as a mere liberal. Indeed, when I conducted a television interview in New York with Norman Podhoretz, editor of *Commentary* and one of the gurus of neoconservatism, he told me that the term "neoliberal" would have been just as logical a label for his movement as "neoconservative."

Whatever its underpinnings, the newly fashioned ideology was a means to deliberately tear up the social contract of the postwar decades. While this was most obvious in the case of Britain, it has been almost as obvious in the United States and Canada. In Britain, the decisive shift took place in the 1970s, with the Conservative Party's rejection of the postwar "consensus," an informal understanding between government, labour, and business that both the Tories and the Labour Party had long accepted. Margaret Thatcher had always hated this consensus and set out to destroy it by crushing the trade unions, ending all consultative procedures in economic policy-making, and limiting the welfare state if it couldn't be eliminated.

Much the same pattern can be seen among the American Republicans in their evolution from Dwight Eisenhower through Barry Goldwater and Richard Nixon to Ronald Reagan and the hapless George Bush. The "modern" Republicanism of Eisenhower, and even Nixon, accepted much of the New Deal and was scorned by conservative critics for being an echo of liberalism rather than a real alternative to it. Goldwater drew a sharp line between himself and liberalism on two counts: he wanted to drastically curtail government spending and the welfare state, and he was an extremely aggressive anticommunist whose goal was to roll back the Soviets rather than merely contain them. By the time Reagan became president, the various strands of the new conservatism had come together. When Reagan fired the striking air traffic controllers, cut taxes, and sharply increased defence spending, the United States had truly entered the promised land of market ideology.

The return of the Democrats to the White House with Bill Clinton does not negate that history, as I will show in the next chapter. For now the point needs to be made that the modern Democratic Party also accepts the fundamentals of the market ideology. Clinton's economic and social programs differ from those of Reagan and Bush; even so, the new president was very careful during the election campaign to reassure Wall Street and the American public that he accepted the basics of market economics. It is best to view Clinton from a global perspective. While the new president differs in many important ways from George Bush, on economic and social issues he is still closer to his Republican predecessor than he is to either the Europeans or the Japanese. Clinton's ideas are variations within an American consensus; under his leadership the American economy will still be overwhelmingly market-driven, and the role of government will remain distinctly secondary.

For neoconservatives, the market is society's most important institution and the best available instrument for generating wealth. Their most important contribution to the politics of globalization is the idea that society should make its basic decisions in the marketplace, leaving only regulatory functions to the state. Their reasoning is that when national governments make important socio-economic decisions—setting priorities for production and consumption, redistributing wealth, or steering research and development—they are interfering with the free play of the market and marring the uniformity of the global economic playing field. In the eyes of those who have fashioned the globalization doctrine, those who would promote market imperfections are heretics. When nation-states were first "invented," they expanded markets by breaking down age-old local barriers to commerce. Now, when a state insists on setting its own rules and on responding to the wishes of its electorate, it is targeted by the neoconservatives as a barrier to efficiency. Investors, businesses, and economists are ever vigilant against such rogue states, insisting that they must be punished so that others will not join them in their outlaw ways. Such vigilance amounts to a direct assault on political democracy.

Neoconservatives acknowledge the contradiction between democratic politics and the market; they also know which side they are on. Against the arguments in favour of national self-determination and political democracy, they reply that the marketplace should be extended as far as possible. Neoconservatives would prefer that people saw themselves as consumers rather than citizens. The concept of citizenship, which owes so much to the Enlightenment and to the revolutions of the eighteenth century, has always contained in it the potential for assertions of radical equality, which involve assaults on inequality and on the rights of property. Neoconservatism, alternatively, is about the reassertion of the legitimacy of inequality.

Neoconservative intellectuals and political leaders have developed the proposition that government is inefficient and that its decisions are inevitably the result of pressures from various special-interest groups. The assumption is that democratically elected governments are less worthy decision-makers than private corporations, which are accountable only to their shareholders. I would reply that in corporate structures, a kind of equality exists, but it is far from the equality in which one person is valued as highly as another. Instead there is an equality in which one dollar is valued as highly as another. "One person, one vote" is replaced by "one dollar, one vote."

Using the argument that they are responding to the dictates of globalization, neoconservatives conduct assaults against minimum-wage and maximum-hour laws, collective bargaining, guaranteed domestic markets for farmers, and social programs that make business costs higher in one jurisdiction than another.

Despite their great influence in our era, neoconservatives have had to face challenges from those even further to the right. I have already made the point that modern-day conservatism has nothing to do with traditional conservative values such as the preservation of communities and historic traditions. I would add here that it is a utilitarian doctrine, a handmaiden for multinational corporations, which embraces no concept of what is good except for the freedom of the market. That has been its strength in negating Marxism, but its weakness against the darker strains of right-wing thought that have been springing up everywhere in the industrialized world in response to the chaos created by globalization.

Neoconservatism does not take into account anything that would reinforce social peace and traditional ways of doing things; instead, propelled by new technology and corporate power, it is advancing a program which is nothing less than the remaking of the world.

The Holy Grail of the conservative agenda is competitiveness; the unintended consequence of the search for it has been havoc. Plants close, the economic base of entire regions is laid waste, small- and medium-sized businesses are taken over or driven into bankruptcy. The business sector stops emphasizing the production of goods and the selling of services, and "money games" become central. Takeovers, leveraged buyouts, junk bonds, and currency speculation are the dubious result of conservative deregulation at both the domestic and the global level. Cost cutting to achieve competitiveness is the domestic equivalent to competitive deflation on the international level. Such strategies did much to create the long recession that began in the major English-speaking countries in 1990 and has been spreading to the rest of the world ever since.

The stepchild of the conservative revolution is the politics of exclusion. Rising unemployment leads to a sharp rise in the number of people who are permanently poor. Violent crime and the dole plague society. Such havoc inspires the search for scapegoats. It is scapegoating that has spawned a new, exclusionist right wing with values that are different from those of market conservatives. Immigrants, visible minorities, AIDS sufferers, homosexuals, and welfare recipients are its targets. The process is far advanced in both North America and Europe.

Everywhere it has arisen, the exclusionist right has threatened the strength of the neoconservatives. While the latter were tearing down walls to free the flow of commerce, their policies pushed up new walls of social division. Now the exclusionists man those ramparts as much against the neoconservatives as everyone else.

REALITIES OF THE NEW GLOBAL AGE

If the globalization hypothesis amounts to special pleading on behalf of powerful vested interests, it remains for us to search out the genuine characteristics of the new global age.

There is no question that the new age is the product of advanced capitalism. We have been so used to hearing that social revolutions are upon us—in the Third World, among women and young people, and so on—that we have difficulty accepting that a sweeping revolution has begun where most of us least expected it—in the heart of the advanced capitalist world.

Capitalism will continue—a point which, while hardly in dispute, is nonetheless critical. Continuity in the world of the late twentieth century will depend on the survival of private enterprise and the market. It must be noted, however, that capitalism is a dynamic system which is constantly evolving and in which competing subsystems are always present. For some time the contest for global power has been an economic contest among these subsystems. That was true even when the Soviet Union still existed. Now that the Soviet system has collapsed, there is no longer any ambiguity about it.

Within the advanced industrial world, the three subsystems —American, European, and Japanese—have each evolved with important features, distinct from those of the other two. As always in the competition among such subsystems, the development of new technology and, just as important, adaptation to the potential offered by new technology, is critical to how things will turn out. "Globalization" is a misnomer for the age in which we live; "multi-polar capitalism" is much more accurate.

Capitalism is characterized by uneven development. Particular business sectors within any given country are always rising and falling relative to other sectors, just as business in any given country is constantly gaining or losing ground relative to business in other countries. Technological development has always propelled capitalism.

Over the past two centuries, particularly prominent new technologies have become the symbols of different world ages. The spinning mule was at the centre of England's cotton industry during the first Industrial Revolution; iron, railways, and steel were the symbols of power in the late nineteenth and early twentieth centuries (which was also the time of the great imperial rivalries); nuclear weaponry for many years symbolized the postwar decades.

Often, when a new technology comes on line, established powers are overtaken by challengers. This happened in the late nineteenth century, when both Germany and the United States overtook Britain in the new age of steel, chemicals, and electrical products. Since the mid-1970s, the microelectronic revolution has swept Japan to the forefront of industrial powers, enabling it to threaten the United States for supremacy, the way Britain was threatened a century ago.

Here are two other cases where countries gained immensely from new technology.

- The rise of new metal industries at the end of the nineteenth century made nickel a strategic resource—a fact of immense importance to northern Ontario, where that metal was found in vast

quantities. Before its hardening property was
needed for warships, airplanes, and structural steel,
nickel had been of little importance.

- The railway age favoured continental countries
  like the United States and Canada, by providing a
  means for developing their mineral deposits and
  vast wheat-growing lands. Without the railways,
  wheat could not have been exported from the heart
  of North America to the rest of the world.

A new technology can be a good match or a bad one for a country's resource endowments, strategic position, and geography. But just as important to economic success are these two factors: the nature of a country's business class, and the way that class and the government work together.

American business has a fixation with quarter-to-quarter bottom lines and has long displayed a deep distrust of innovation. It has relied on the great gains it made during the Second World War, and much prefers to copy from its competitors rather than seek genuine innovations. The drawbacks to innovation are that it forces the destruction of existing capital and requires enormous up-front investment, and that a very long time must pass before any profits are seen. A business class that prefers accountants and lawyers to engineers and other hands-on people does not usually seek involvement in long-term innovative ventures. The career patterns of North American business executives reinforce this tendency to chase short-term gains. American executives are judged by their ability to increase profits quickly. They also change companies frequently during their careers. This is in contrast to Japanese executives, for whom lifetime employment is the pattern. In North America, by the time the positive results are felt from a long-term investment, the executive who backed it has likely moved to another company—if he or she hasn't been terminated in favour of another who is adept at corporate takeovers and mergers, which are more profitable in the short term. In the United States this has truly been the age of the paper entrepreneur.

State intervention can definitely give business an edge in exploiting new technology. A very good example of this was the Japanese strategy for developing microelectronics, which without a doubt is the critical innovative technology in the new global age. Microelectronics has changed the nature of manufacturing, has revolutionized the way firms run offices and handle inventory, and has enabled a transformation of the way financial services are performed on a global basis.

In Japan both business and the state were heavily involved in developing the microelectronics sector. The state relaxed the anti-cartel rules so that companies could conduct basic research together and develop new product lines. Later these companies resumed fierce competition in marketing their own products. The state also underwrote low-interest loans to smaller Japanese businesses so that they could purchase or lease the computer-driven robots that Japanese industry had developed. In 1985, at the height of this development, I visited a leasing outlet in Tokyo that had geared itself to making the latest robots comprehensible and available to small businesses. Such rental-leasing arrangements helped the industry to thrive.

Once the Japanese had successfully developed their home market, they were in a very strong position to move into external markets. Meanwhile, at home, economies of scale had given them an advantage over foreign competitors.

Microelectronics did more than propel the Japanese assault on American power; it also did serious harm to the industrial world's working class, and perhaps ultimately to Marxism, the ideology that was predicated on the inevitable triumph of the working class. The second Industrial Revolution, that of the late nineteenth century, assembled the working class in huge battalions in enormous workplaces; microelectronics has dispersed, divided, and reduced the size of the working class. It has also reduced the size of the work force through robotics and other innovations, while profoundly changing its nature. Many skilled trades are now disappearing, while a few others are blossoming and in heavy demand.

Hundreds of workers in every auto assembly plant have been replaced by robots that are much more adept than humans at such tasks as painting and spot welding. By taking power away from many workers while giving new power to a smaller number, microelectronics, at least for now, has seriously undermined the solidarity of wage earners. It has also established a new aristocracy of technologically literate labour. The workers in this group do not consider their interests to be the same as those of the older, more heavily unionized sectors.

The new technology has also customized manufacturing. With the help of computers, companies can now produce "one off" items as easily as they used to produce identical ones. For example, auto factories I have visited in North

America and Europe have computerized assembly lines. A computer printout accompanies each vehicle through the line, listing the particular accessories that are to be added so that each finished product may be very different from the last. This is the opposite of what was done on Henry Ford's original assembly lines; the strength of those was that every car made was exactly the same, and therefore cheaper to make—and for the consumer to buy.

Unlike the Americans, the Japanese have invested huge amounts of capital to deploy microelectronics on a very large scale. At the same time, they have trained and deployed a work force that is more technologically literate than the American one. Though it has only half the population, Japan trains as many engineers as the United States. Japanese factories are staffed with workers who are capable of using highly sophisticated technology to its full capacity. American outrage over the fact that microelectronics was first developed in the United States cannot detract from the Japanese success at exploiting it much more thoroughly than anyone else.

Microelectronics has also provided the basis for a revolution in global financial services. This is the age of footloose capital. Capital can now be shifted from continent to continent at the flick of a cursor. Markets operate twenty-four hours a day as trading shifts from Tokyo to London to New York. Never before have capital flows vastly exceeded the value of commodities being traded.

Of course, this revolution is also the result of government policies—such as the widespread deregulation of markets and the removal of capital controls—that have exploited the technology for particular purposes. Linda McQuaig offers a useful caution against technological determinism when she writes that "there is little natural connection between the dramatic changes brought on by the computer revolution and neoconservative policies." [2] For example, the present plague of currency speculation in the world's financial system, while a result of neoconservative deregulation, is hardly an inevitable use of new technology.

State intervention has been vital to Japan's success in microelectronics. A similar state-supported assault on the technological high ground has been mounted by European governments in the aerospace sector. The governments of Germany, France, Britain, and Spain have underwritten the Airbus consortium for more than twenty years. By the beginning of the 1990s, Airbus had won a one-third share of the world's civilian aircraft market. So angered have the Americans been by this state-assisted support for a company that is taking crucial markets from Boeing and McDonnell Douglas, which are the major American aerospace firms, that placing limits on government support for Airbus has been one of the two key items on the Americans' agenda in their negotiations with the European Community. (The other key item is agricultural subsidies.)

The advantages gained from the successful exploitation of new technology are no small matter: they can critically strengthen the relative position of business in particular countries at the expense of foreign competitors.

Real economic gains are by nature long-term. Manufacturing virtuosity results in increased exports. The earnings that flow from those exports help countries to build up their capital assets so that they can eventually become lenders of capital to other countries. At the apex of the international division of labour are the exporters of capital. It is no accident that as American manufacturing has faltered, the United States has gone from being the world's largest creditor nation to its largest debtor. The Americans' failure to fully deploy new technology has been central to this result.

Global trading is closely related to the rise of global corporations. These are based in particular countries but operate in many parts of the world, mobilizing capital and labour, undertaking research and development, pursuing markets, and shifting their tax burdens to maximize their overall advantage. The annual revenues of the biggest multinationals are often as large as the GDPs of medium-sized industrial countries.

In the new global age, multinational corporations play a formidable role in the goods-producing and financial services sectors of the economy. Largely because of the position of the multinationals, there has been a profound blurring of national markets, with the result that most states have suffered a loss of effective sovereignty. Most nations can no longer set the economic and social agendas within their own boundaries. American economist Robert Reich, now Secretary of Labor in the Clinton administration, makes the interesting point that in the new global age, only a country's infrastructure and the skills of its work force remain national. Technology and capital can migrate anywhere.

In the industrialized world in the new global age, only a few countries will be global economic engines, generating demand and dictating the overall level of economic activity. The others will be forced into a supplier role, pressured to adapt to the general trends established by the engine economies.

As we enter the new age, ideologies, social forces, and institutional arrangements that we have taken for granted in the twentieth century are now in doubt. Marxism, the industrial working class, and national self-determination used to be seen as representing the future. Now they appear to represent the past. Those with vested interests in these movements and ideas, which are so close to the heart of the twentieth century, naturally enough are the first to denounce the very idea of a new age. What is most telling, however, is how much these people have changed their attitude towards the future. They once believed that the future meant inevitable victory for them; now they stress continuity, insisting that much of what they once believed in is still relevant. Their sea change with respect to the future is itself hard evidence that a new age has begun.

All of these technological, economic, and social transformations are central to the new global era but are not the only evidence that it has begun. The postwar age, which has now ended, rested on a bipolar system of global power in which the United States and to a lesser extent the Soviet Union dominated the world. The collapse of the Soviet Union and its satellite states has, of course, been the most dramatic development of our time. Another central event, directly related to the first, has been the unification of Germany, around which a new European superpower is taking shape. Similarly, though it continues to emphasize its economic power and to reject a leading political role, Japan has grown immensely in global power, and will continue to do so over the next several decades. Meanwhile, the United States, as I will show in the next chapter, is finding its global preeminence challenged by the ascending stars of Europe and Japan.

If I had to pick a moment when the bipolar world gave way to the new age of multi-polar capitalism, I would offer November 9, 1989, the day the East German government gave in to its citizens' demands and opened the Berlin Wall. The Soviet and American global positions in the postwar era had both been anchored in Berlin, so the revolution in East Germany signalled the end of the postwar era and changed the global balance of power. It prepared the way not only for the rapid unification of Germany but also for an end to the foreign military presence in Europe—the Russians would withdraw quickly and the Americans would soon begin phasing themselves out. The opening of the Berlin Wall was a huge step towards the complete collapse of Moscow's empire in eastern Europe and towards the disintegration of the Soviet Union itself.

The fall of the Soviet Union in late 1991 left the United States as the only superpower, yet at the same time threatened its global position. Without the Cold War to enforce solidarity among the leading non-communist industrial powers, the Americans' authority to act as the unquestioned leaders of the free world was suddenly in doubt. Europe (centred on Germany) and Japan were well positioned to carve out vast new power for themselves.

The conclusion that a new age has begun rests on all of these technological, economic, and geopolitical changes. Their combined impact has been to alter the preoccupations of humanity, so that the assumptions and approaches of the age that has passed can no longer be used to grapple with the future. The final proof that a new age is upon us is found in the widespread recognition that the world must now be rethought.

STATES AND MARKETS

The very bedrock of the age that has now ended was an institution which had been at the centre of political economy for two centuries—the nation-state. For as long as human beings have organized societies, there have been sovereign states. However, the kind of sovereign state we now take for granted—the nation-state—is a comparatively recent invention. Today it is still the "ideal" form of statehood for most peoples, as well as the norm against which all political systems measure themselves. Even so, nation-states face unique pressures that challenge their capacity to play their accustomed role.

Most of our present ideas about the obligations of the nation-state were formed in the decades that followed the Second World War. During those decades, which were an economic golden age throughout the industrialized world, the state assumed responsibilities for social and educational programs in what amounted to a social revolution.

The word "revolution" needs to be justified in this case. The era from the late 1940s to the mid-1970s was unlike any other in social and economic history. It was the longest period of sustained economic growth ever, and a time when most people in the advanced industrial world gained a stake in prosperity. When the era began, most people were poor; by the time it ended, most were not. This new majority had acquired housing, mobility, the benefits of instant communications, a varied diet, and the prospects of a better education for their children. And in varying degrees, depending on the country in which they lived, they had become recipients of social programs such as health care, unemployment insurance, pension plans, wider state support for education, and subsidized child care. The result of these changes was increased life expectancy, a dramatic decline in poverty among the elderly, and the expectation that living standards would continue to improve into the next generation.

During these decades, the nation-states of the advanced industrial world had become, in varying degrees, social states, the guarantors of minimum standards for everyone. These states had committed themselves to demand-side economics, according to which full employment is a central goal. There were several reasons for this new commitment—the postwar compromise between business and labour, the weakness of conservatism following the defeat of fascism, and the continuing rise of mass-production industrialism.

Yet a paradox lay at the heart of the system. The achievements of the welfare state generated nationalist pride in many countries. But while the emergence of state welfare programs suggested that the capacity for vital decision-making was found at the nation-state level, the real authority for managing the global economy was concentrated in the United States. The system turned on unresolved tensions between the nation-states and the Americans. The former wanted to maintain their social and economic autonomy; the latter wanted to subordinate the nation-states to the principles of the Bretton Woods international system, under which the United States would guide the free world's economy.

In the era that began with the French Revolution, the nation-state was the ideal structure for giving life to the radical new concepts of the time. Central among these was the idea of citizenship, whereby participation in the political process was no longer to be limited to a tiny hereditary élite. Citizenship and democracy were the new banners under which the new middle classes could march to power. The emerging nation-states provided the context in which these ideas could be realized.

At the end of the twentieth century, the world is crowded with nation-states. But how much sovereignty do most of them now possess? Paradoxically, although the number of nation-states is continuing to rise, real sovereignty has been shifting to different entities. The multinational corporations, in deploying the era's new technology, have established a new global economy, and in so doing have substantially narrowed the freedom of action of most sovereign states. The emergence of a global financial market has had the same effect. Many nation-states have been reduced to virtual "administrators," carrying out the will of the global economic system, which is where the decisions are now made.

Neoconservatives often portray the decline of the state as a central feature of our age. However, such a view is a fundamental misreading of what is, in fact, a system of multi-polar capitalism. Consider the two most important myths surrounding the globalization hypothesis.

- We are witnessing the onset of a borderless world in which the state is becoming less important.
- All states are losing power more or less equally as a consequence of globalization.

Putting aside for the moment the special pleas that neo-conservatives often make on behalf of the first myth, the genuine confusion here has to do with the changing role of the state in an era of economic and social transformation. Especially in the Anglo-American world, globalization is associated with the decline of the state because of the types of policies being adopted by governments in response to competitive pressures. As I have already noted, the Anglo-American response to the challenge of rising exports from Japan, Germany, and the newly industrializing countries was to try to cut the cost of government by slashing social programs, or at least hold the line on increases in social spending. Associated with this was the rejection of industrial strategy. Thatcherism and Reaganism both rejected corporatism, which involves business, labour, and the state reaching a consensus on economic policy.[3]

As far as neoconservatives were concerned, the external challenge had a very welcome aspect—it drastically reduced the bargaining power of labour. Instead of promoting a social partnership with labour, they proposed allowing the marketplace to shake out the winners and losers. If that meant long periods of high unemployment, at least the power of the unions would be weakened, which would have the welcome effect of subjecting domestic workers to competition from workers in lower-wage countries.

This cost-cutting, market-centred response to contemporary pressures has been widely followed in the English-
speaking world, whatever political parties have held power.
But it ignores the fact that other advanced countries have taken
an altogether different approach to the new global economic
terrain. In economic matters, Japan and most leading western
European countries, including Germany, have continued to
practise much more government intervention than is seen in
Britain and the United States. Such intervention has taken a
number of forms—the provision of capital for domestically
owned industrial "champions," state subsidies for research and
development, large-scale public investment in infrastructure,
targeted tax incentives for business, and, particularly in France
and Italy, large-scale public ownership. In every case the goal
has been to make up for the perceived deficiencies of
unchained market economics.

The economic battles fought between states are more
intense now than ever before. Some weapons in the state arse-
nals have become obsolete, but new ones are always being
developed. We are witnessing a wildly uneven process that
involves gigantic shifts in power from country to country—that
gives some states immense new leverage and leaves others
with very little room to manoeuvre. Tariffs are not much used
any more, but anti-dumping duties are alive and well. Broad
economic planning has declined in importance, but many
states still work very aggressively to subsidize, capitalize, and
protect key industrial firms, especially if these are seen as the
means for dominating the critical industries of the future.

In making sense of multi-polar capitalism, the most

profound error we can make is to believe that we are going to live in a borderless world, with the state put into retirement. The state remains central to how things will turn out. What *has* changed is the way in which the state will now play the game of influencing economic outcomes, in tandem with multinational corporations.

The losers in the struggle for economic power will have their power stripped away and become dependent on others; the winners will gain vast new global authority. In some cases—the European Community being by far the most important one—regional groups of states will pool their economic and political sovereignty to create new federations, which themselves will become powerful global states. There are very solid reasons for believing that the biggest loser in this process will be the United States, the only remaining superpower as the new age begins.

THE DILEMMA OF NATIONALISM

If a state can no longer make basic choices, how can its citizens expect their votes to matter when they elect their governments? Sovereignty, which involves the right to decide fundamental questions, has been revealed in today's world to be anything but secure. Crucial decisions are now made by a bewildering array of public and private interests; some are made within the jurisdiction of nation-states, but many now outside. Most nation-states are losing much of their sovereignty, with the result that their citizens are growing angry and bewildered—unable to understand how decisions are being made and whom they should hold accountable. Throughout the democratic world, politicians are being viewed with increasing cynicism—even contempt—by electorates that see the old certitudes of national life slipping away.

What implications does this loss of sovereignty have for democracy? If a "democratic deficit" of serious proportions has emerged, how can this be addressed by democrats?

Contemporary developments have reduced the effectiveness of economic nationalism. The rising power of multinational corporations in this era of footloose capital has severely limited the nation-states' powers to set their own economic and social agendas. If economic nationalism has lost much of its strength, what of the potential for supranationalism, whereby the peoples of a number of countries join together to pursue a linked social agenda? Supranationalism, which is the political counterpart to multinational corporations, copes with the new age on its own terrain. In doing so it by no means undermines the cultural, social, or political aspirations of regions and nations. Indeed, in many respects, it provides a framework for realizing those aspirations.

Nationalism's great strength has been its capacity to nurture solidarity within a given culture. Such solidarity can be vital to the achieving of social goals, such as the building of a welfare state. In this sense, nationalism has acted as a brake on the efforts of the multinationals to impose a monolithic social agenda.

Nationalism's greatest weakness has been that, by definition, it does not permit the building of effective political coalitions with people from other nations. In some cases, nationalists actually view such coalitions as unprincipled. These drawbacks, which are a consequence of the we–they dichotomy that is central to all forms of nationalism, have left nationalists weak beyond the boundaries of their own separate nations. This has done much to strengthen the hand of the multinationals.

In these opening days of the new age, we recognize that much has already been stolen from us. So that corporations and the marketplace can operate unfettered on a global basis, it has been necessary to curtail the sovereignty of nation-states. Also, our citizenship has lost much of its lustre. The new age has begun with the destruction of much that has long provided identity and political strength to the peoples of the advanced industrial world—but it need not continue this way.

Neoconservatives and multinationals have set out to reorder the world in their own image, for their own purposes. Those whom they have dispossessed will now have to act forcefully to win back what they have lost—that being membership in a meaningful political community which can base its decisions on the assumption that all people are equal rather than on the rule of capital.

There is a new global age, but its characteristics are not those claimed by the proponents of globalization. In fact, globalization is a divisive, dead-end response to an era of multipolar capitalism. Two great risks confront Canadians. One is that we may "buy" globalization, the neoconservative version of change; the other is that we may deny the reality of a new global age and in doing so fail to comprehend the profound changes that are indeed sweeping the world.

CHAPTER TWO

AN AGE OF AMERICAN
DECLINE

Shortly after he led his party to victory in the September 1984 federal election, Brian Mulroney addressed the Economic Club of New York, where he declared that Canada was once again "open for business." The statement meant more than that Canada was about to adopt an uncritically favourable attitude to American investment; what it really meant was that Canada was adopting the United States as its economic and social role model. Brian Mulroney was speaking from the heart—the rich in the United States were fattening at the trough under Ronald Reagan, and we Canadians wanted in on it. We were no longer going to be content with watching from the other side of the border.

It has been the policy of the Conservative government and the overwhelming preference of the business class to regard the United States as the promised land. The persistent goal of those who have ruled Canada since 1984 has been to make Canada ever more like its southern neighbour.

That preoccupation on the part of those who have held power makes it essential for us to ask these questions: just what kind of promised land is the United States? And should

Canadians fall in behind the Americans on their route march towards their economic and social destination?

In this chapter, I will make the case that Canadians should refuse, as they always have, to try the American experiment.

When the Americans chose Bill Clinton as their president, they took an important step away from the exaggerated right-wing rhetoric, and the overt favouritism towards the rich, that had so characterized the orgiastic age of Ronald Reagan and its sputtering denouement under George Bush. Clinton's victory gave hope to those who had been so patently ignored by his predecessors, who simply hadn't acknowledged the America of the inner cities, of fifty million blacks and Hispanics, of the millions who live in poverty. It reasserted the existence and importance of these Americans. But hope and good will, while they do matter, do not in themselves generate a social transformation, especially when the man who inspired them has never promised vast changes.

With Clinton, Americans have edged back towards moderation, but without changing their fundamental assumptions about politics, the economy, or society. While they are prepared to regard active government more favourably than before, their move in this direction is modest—a corrective within an overall American approach to society and the economy that Clinton is not going to change. The new president differs from Reagan and Bush in favouring limited government action to help preserve society; but he still adheres to the orthodox American idea that the marketplace ought to be at the centre of that society.

Clinton's liberalism sits within the central framework of

Americanism. The new president is a self-proclaimed moderate who has set out to lead the Democratic Party back to the American mainstream that had been abandoned by ideological liberals like George McGovern and Michael Dukakis. The assumptions of his presidency might be called "conservative liberalism" or, just as logically, "liberal conservatism." In any case, he represents a centrist American tendency and not a new approach, as will be clear when we observe how much his views on the economy and society differ from those of the Europeans and the Japanese.

Just what are the basic assumptions of the American approach to governance? While the American mainstream has often been labelled conservative, its ideas have little to do with classical conservatism. In fact, at the centre of American "conservatism" is the commitment to a market-driven society with limited government and a very limited social contract. A right-wing variant of this, dedicated to reducing the tax burden of the rich, was represented by Ronald Reagan. A moderate variant is represented by Bill Clinton, who believes in more government activism in infrastructure renewal and the educational system.

Clinton is no social democrat, nor does he believe in an industrial policy along Japanese or European lines. In the area of social policy—which includes the critical issue of health care—his administration's approach is far less activist than that of any Christian democratic or social democratic regime in western Europe, not to mention Canada.

Indeed, Clinton looks like a liberal only when compared with his strongly right-wing predecessors. On matters such as abortion, abortion counselling, and the rights of gays, the new president is pointedly more liberal than were Reagan and Bush. But on the more expensive and therefore more difficult questions—health care, social welfare, and infrastructure—he is clearly a moderate. Early in his presidency, Clinton proposed modest tax increases to curtail the federal deficit and to undertake new spending in key areas. On the basis of this program, no one should expect him to accomplish the rebuilding of American cities, infrastructure, and schools.

It also needs to be noted that some of Clinton's appeal in the American suburbs was based on a set of ideas with which Reagan would have been comfortable—an unswerving support for the death penalty, a tough stance against crime, and a pledge to put 100,000 more police officers on America's streets. Indeed, Clinton was one of the few Democratic governors to support Reagan's covert war in Nicaragua. He displayed a harsh-edged American nationalism during the election campaign by signalling his intention to look out for American interests with little regard for the interests of others.

Within the advanced industrial world, the United States remains very much an island unto itself. The American political and social system is highly self-contained in the sense that Americans, unlike almost everyone else on the planet, very rarely look abroad for comparisons with others, against which to judge themselves. Indeed, it is no exaggeration to suggest that Americans, even members of élites, typically display a shockingly limited knowledge of the rest of the world. That condition of separateness colours American understanding of historical change and of the onset of a new global age. Americans tend to see the world through an ideological prism which limits and distorts their perception of what is happening.

In the end, it was the seemingly endless recession that destroyed the presidency of George Bush. During his four years in office, Bush compiled the worst economic record of any postwar president. Yet it should not be forgotten that before his defeat in November 1992, he had once soared as high in public esteem as any president ever has. His demise tells us much about the United States; but so did his moment of glory.

Triumphalism is the mind-set of the victor, the purest public expression of self-indulgence. Americans wallowed in triumphalism as they watched communism collapse, first in eastern Europe and later in the Soviet Union itself. In the winter of 1991, while its Cold War enemy was disintegrating, the United States won its first military victory since the Second World War. The free market had prevailed against communism, while "smart" weapons had easily overcome Saddam Hussein's massed infantry. All of this inspired endless triumphalist proclamations by American public figures, this one by James R. Schlesinger, a former CIA director, being representative of the lot. He was writing about the opening of the Berlin Wall: "For 40 years we have stood the watch. We have won. I say this not in the spirit of gloating but as a historical fact."[1]

My own most intense exposure to triumphalism came in mid-March 1991, when I drove two thousand miles up and down the eastern seaboard of the United States over a ten-day span. The Gulf War had just ended. General Norman Schwarzkopf was at the height of his fame. Everywhere I went, patriotic fervour clouded the air. Along Interstate 95, where billboards provide most of the scenery, motorists were running a gauntlet of praise for the U.S. military: American flags and yellow ribbons were everywhere. At one service station southeast of Washington, military personnel were offered a discount on gasoline, and soft drink cases were piled up so that their colours fashioned the American flag.

All along the route, towns and cities were cheering the return of units from the Persian Gulf. Cars and pickup trucks sported flags and yellow ribbons and hand-lettered signs supporting the American armed forces. At truck stops I sometimes saw men wearing desert-style military fatigues. The yellow ribbons created the impression of a cult group—of a brotherhood of sorts—and it was easy to identify its headquarters. Over the front door of the White House was a giant yellow wreath—the yellow ribbon to end all yellow ribbons. But what impressed me most was the astonishing outpouring of patriotism in the grimy, depressing rust belt cities of eastern Pennsylvania. An hour's drive from Philadelphia, in one section of one decaying city, no fewer than forty per cent of the tattered frame houses had flags decorating their front windows.

Not once among all the symbols, ribbons, flags, and slogans did I see a reference to Kuwait, the emirate on whose behalf the war was presumably fought, or to the United Nations, which had authorized the use of military force, or to the allies, who ostensibly were fashioning the new world order alongside the United States. All of the emotion was directed inward: Americans were speaking to other Americans and to no one else. They were exorcising the ghosts of Vietnam. This was nationalism unalloyed.

When one considers the public goals that American policymakers had been setting for themselves since the onset of the Cold War, this triumphalism is understandable. In a speech in mid-1947, William C. Bullitt of the U.S. State Department concluded that "the final aim of Russia is world conquest."[2] Some months earlier, in March of the same year, Harry Truman had declared that America's goal was to resist communist expansionism everywhere in the world. In putting forward what came to be called the Truman Doctrine, he stated that "it must be the policy of the United States to support free peoples who are resisting attempted subjugation by armed minorities or by outside pressures."[3]

The Cold War was not approached in simple balance-of-power terms, as had been the competition among the great European powers in the late nineteenth century. For Americans, it was a twilight struggle between good and evil, a battle of absolutes. As late as the fall of 1985, when the Soviet state was already disintegrating, Irving Kristol was still able to proclaim in a neoconservative journal that "in our own era, the distinction between religious ideas and political ideas is blurred ... We live in an era of 'ideologies'—of political ideas that breathe quasi-religious aspirations and involve quasi-religious commitments ... The basic conflict of our times—that between the USSR and the United States—is ideological."[4]

Such a holy cause demanded a single-minded commitment, so when the Soviet state and its ruling ideology crumbled to dust, the Americans' sense of triumph was total. But this total sense of triumph was symptomatic of a total lack of perspective. During the decades of the Cold War, to understand the world from a bipolar perspective, U.S.A. versus U.S.S.R., always involved an oversimplification. To continue to see the world that way in the mid-1980s, as Irving Kristol did, was the sort of blindness to which most Americans were prone. Even as communism was collapsing, Americans were underestimating very important world developments, simply because they did not fit their Cold War mind-set.

When the Soviet Union collapsed, the United States was the only world power left from the great partnership that won the Second World War. The British Empire had crumbled in the decade and a half after that war. Now only the United States remained as the symbol of order and continuity for a world in transition.

Powers that have won a great victory are loathe to change their ways and are not adept at analyzing the risks that face them. Victory in the Cold War has reinforced a powerful tendency in American society not to look to the rest of the world for ideas. Essentially, Americans have not questioned their assumption that the American way is the best way. Contemporary American political and social orthodoxy rests on certain axioms that are very rarely examined. Stripped down, those axioms are these.

- Capitalism is in tune with humanity's essential nature, which at heart is individualist and acquisitive.
- Competitive market capitalism, with a minimum of state intervention, is the best way to organize an economy.
- The United States, the supreme nation-state, is

and should remain a law unto itself, intervening in
the world whenever its interests are threatened,
but never conceding sovereignty to the wider
global community.

Liberals and conservatives have fought over a wide
variety of issues in the United States; however, these axioms
are shared by all of mainstream America.

The United States, the last superpower, now finds itself
confronting a world turned upside down, one in which the
nations it did much to defeat in 1945 are now at the heart of
the two most successful economic systems in this new global
era. These two nations are, of course, Japan, which is the
central player in rising East Asia, and Germany, which is the
driving engine of the European Community.

The collapse of the Soviet Union and the rise of Europe
and Japan should be reason enough for the United States to
reevaluate its global position. There is, however, an even more
compelling reason—a deepening domestic crisis that is bound
to alter the ability of Americans to respond effectively to their
powerful new competitors.

THE AMERICAN CRISIS

An American crisis has been developing since the 1960s. It is
a result of social, political, and economic problems which have
woven themselves into a knot of persistent difficulties that
strongly resists untangling. This crisis has global significance,
as I will now show.

The Cold War had always been based on a bitter rivalry between the Soviet Union and the United States. The latter was always able to count on its allies—western Europe, Japan, and others—to support the main precepts of American global authority. Much less obvious, but extremely important, was the fact that the relationship between the two superpowers also involved a joint dominion. This was clearest in the case of Germany: American and Soviet forces occupied that divided country and its most important city throughout the Cold War. Lord Ismay, the first secretary-general of NATO, saw his organization's *raison d'être* as being "to keep the U.S. in, the Soviet Union out and Germany down"—a perfect summary of the Cold War's real purpose.

Virtually until the collapse of the Soviet Union, Americans rarely thought about the benefits the Cold War brought them. This, even though it provided the ideal climate for fostering American global power. The Cold War allowed the United States to mobilize the energies of both its citizens and its allies. For this, the Soviet Union was the ideal opponent: its "socialist" system was actually a state-centred tyranny that by the end of the 1920s had lost all vestiges of socialist humanism; and with its glaring socio-economic weaknesses, it could never succeed in dominating the world. Ironically, therefore, its collapse turned out to be the greatest threat to confront the United States since the Second World War. Europe and Japan, no longer on the front lines of a global alliance against communism, could now radically transform their relationship with the United States; they could be expected to consider their own interests first and American sensibilities later. And Europe and

Japan, unlike the Soviet Union, were fully capable of challenging the global position of the United States.

The first truth of the age of multi-polar capitalism, from an American standpoint, is that the competitive struggle with Europe and Japan will be much fiercer than before. How effectively will the Americans meet this challenge? This question takes us back to the "American crisis."

At its heart, the American crisis is about inequality.

The deep structural inequalities that affect every aspect of American life began with the institution of slavery, which made African Americans a permanent "other" in American life. The divisions that slavery created have never been resolved. They continue today, not as a less important feature of American life, but so as to accelerate the crisis in the radically transformed circumstances of an urban society that is going through an unprecedented technological revolution. Racial inequality is a central, not a peripheral feature of American life. It does far more than prevent minorities from fully participating in American society; it also fundamentally harms the social, political, and economic existence of the majority.

The racial divisions of American life, which were only partially addressed in the 1950s and 1960s, have hastened the onset of a wide-ranging socio-economic crisis that is most obvious in the larger American cities. Affluent Americans have recoiled from the problems of the cities and fled to their suburbs. There they have developed an attitude towards the state and society that is highly individualistic and holds out little hope that there will be any collective effort to deal with America's social problems. They focus on their immediate surroundings and insist on paying the lowest taxes of any major industrialized nation. This affluent majority is inclined to regard the problems of the urban poor as a matter for policing rather than for expensive social and educational policies which, though they might transform the country, would undoubtedly mean higher taxes.

Most Americans have been brought up to believe that their country is the most egalitarian in the world; they would dismiss out of hand the idea that their society harbours deeper and more rigid inequalities than any other in the Western world. The reason for the gap between the oft-proclaimed ideal, which holds that the United States is freer from class divisions than any other country, and the reality, which is that minorities are generally locked out of the American mainstream, is that most whites do not really count blacks and Hispanics as true Americans. This has vast implications for all Americans, which I will examine soon. First, however, let us consider the fate of the twenty per cent of Americans who are black or Hispanic.

Neither group has been accepted by American society as fully as European or even Asian immigrants. Instead, new forms of social segregation, enforced less through the legal than through the economic system, have walled off access to the mainstream for both groups. It is accurate to look on the United States as comprising three societies—three nations, as some would have it—the whites, the blacks, and the Hispanics. These three societies are not remotely endowed with equality of opportunity, condition, or power.

Blacks and Hispanics are not evenly distributed across the United States. There are proportionately more blacks in the South, in the core cities of the Northeast and Midwest, and in the big cities of California. As well, Hispanics are a far from homogeneous group. If they live in New York they likely have a Puerto Rican or Dominican background; if they live in Miami they or their parents were probably born in Cuba. Mexicans constitute the largest and fastest-growing group of Hispanics in America. In the great crescent of the Southwest, which includes Texas, New Mexico, Arizona, and southern California, their numbers have increased enormously and will likely keep doing so.

While the rise of Hispanics is a major contemporary fact of American demography, the classic division in American society has been between blacks and whites. Political scientist Andrew Hacker certainly sees it that way.[5] He writes that white America has always stretched its concept of itself to embrace, at least to a degree, successive waves of immigrants, but has been unwilling to do the same for blacks.

At the end of the Second World War, most blacks still lived in the South. During the postwar decades, in one of the great migrations of American history, millions of them moved to the industrial cities of the Northeast and Midwest. Detroit and Chicago were the classic destinations, but there were dozens of lesser ones. Blacks were drawn north by the prospect of relatively high-paying jobs; and in these last decades of the age of American industrial supremacy, hundreds of thousands found them. With the door leading out of segregation open a crack, the cities of the Northeast and Midwest were transformed. But opportunities were still limited, in that white society would not allow blacks to follow other ethnics into mainstream American life.

That separate societies continue today is obvious. Overwhelmingly, the two races continue to live apart. Blacks have also been the victims of a socio-economic transformation that has pulled the ladder to success up and away from them. American economic policies, the arrival of tough competitors in the global economy, the technological revolution, and a demographic shift towards the Sunbelt have all contributed to the steep decline of what was once the greatest industrial region of the entire world. The transformation of the Northeast and Midwest from industrial dynamo to rust belt was an economic event of global significance that also threatened the gains made by those blacks who had moved north.

Although a much larger black middle class emerged between the 1960s and 1990s, most blacks were unable to improve their lives. Indeed, on the whole, the position of blacks relative to whites deteriorated throughout this period. In constant dollars, the median income of black families in the United States increased by only a tiny amount between 1970 and 1990, from $21,151 to $21,423[6]; while that of white families increased somewhat more, from $34,481 to $36,915.[7]

The desperate situation of so many blacks is symptomatic of the increasing social inequality that has marked American life over the past twenty years. The victory of neoconservatism, which seeks to legitimize inequality, has coincided with the actual fact of growing inequality. Evidence that social inequality in the United States has deepened in our time is easy to find. Here are a few good proofs of it.

- The gap between rich and poor widened between 1977 and 1989, with 60 per cent of the increase in

after-tax income going to the richest 1 per cent of
families. At the same time, the bottom 40 per cent
of families suffered declines in income.[8]

- Even though the United States spends more of its
GDP on health care than any other country, so
many Americans have no medical insurance that
infant mortality rates are higher in the United
States than in other developed countries. A very
good example: Greece spends half as much per
capita on health care as the United States yet has a
lower rate of infant mortality.[9]

- The proportion of children living below the
poverty line grew from 14.9 to 19 per cent between
1970 and 1989; in the latter year 43.2 per cent of
black children lived below the poverty line.[10]

- More and more Americans are moving out of the
middle class—some of them towards poverty,
some towards wealth. In 1969, 71 per cent of
Americans lived on middle incomes; by 1989,
this figure was 63 per cent. In 1979, 31 per cent of
American households had an annual income of
less than $25,000; by 1989 this figure had risen
to 42 per cent.[11]

Gaping disparities—between rich and poor, between
gutted inner cities and prosperous suburbs, between regions of
industrial decline and regions in a strong position to deploy
new technologies—have corroded Americans' belief that they
constitute a single people who can work together effectively.

Some blame the new malaise on what they see as a malevolent denial of the commonality of the American experience. In *The Disuniting of America*, the liberal historian Arthur Schlesinger Jr. bewails the tendency of Americans to emphasize their separate ethnic identities; he believes that this takes away much from the common American identity.[12] Schlesinger wants Americans to remember their shared accomplishments of the past so that they can lay a more solid basis for their future; however, the facts of American demography and the sharp fissures in the country's social structure suggest that his solution is faulty. When I conducted a television interview with him in New York in 1980, he had already developed his idea that the United States oscillates between periods of activist liberalism and privatist conservatism. He would see Clinton's victory of 1992 as the beginning of a new period of activism; however, the dramatic evolution of American society towards greater structural inequality will be hard to reverse, as the failed presidency of Jimmy Carter so eloquently demonstrated.

What was being consolidated in the United States in the 1970s and 1980s was an ideology of small government—an ideology that consumed not only the American right but much of the Democratic Party as well. This reworking of American mainstream thought, which involved a rejection of New Deal traditions, was the great achievement of modern-day conservatism. It ensured that large-scale government initiatives would not be taken to grapple with the problems of poverty and urban decay. American conservatives were fundamentally opposed to the kinds of programs that were and still are needed to create and sustain a social transformation. The central ideas of the conservatives were that there was already too much government and that government cost too much. The liberal wars on poverty had been a failure, these people asserted. For them the solution was to encourage private enterprise among blacks and Hispanics instead of extending the welfare state.

THE POLITICAL USES OF RACISM

When a great wave of rioting swept across Los Angeles in April 1992 in response to the acquittal of four white police officers in the beating of Rodney King, an America that had been half-hidden during the glory days of Reagan-style conservatism was thrust back into view. That notorious acquittal provoked the greatest urban explosion of the century in the United States. It left fifty-five people dead, thousands injured and arrested, and one billion dollars of property damage across south-central Los Angeles and other parts of the city. The Watts riots of the mid-1960s had been much smaller in every respect.

Even more chilling than the death toll during the riots is that on average, each week, there are twenty-five murders in Los Angeles. A strong case can be made that a civil war—albeit an anarchic and apolitical one—has been bubbling beneath the surface of American life. In any other industrial country a murder rate as high as America's would long have been understood as a civil war. In 1988, 22,032 people were murdered in the United States, a rate of 9.0 per 100,000. (Canada's 657 murders in 1989 made for a murder rate of 2.5 per 100,000.)[13]

Homicide in the United States is not an even-handed phenomenon. It is highly concentrated in specific urban, social, gender, and racial settings. Blacks are much more likely to be murdered than whites, men much more likely than women. In 1988 the murder rate for black men was a staggering 58.0 per 100,000. For black women the figure was 13.2. Among white men and white women the rates were 7.9 and 2.9 respectively. That murder rates in large cities are much higher than else-where is seen in the following figures for 1988: Detroit, 60.0; Washington, D.C., 71.9; Miami, 34.6; New Orleans, 47.5; New York, 25.8; Los Angeles, 25.5; Chicago, 24.8.[14]

To live with violence has become second nature to Amer-icans. Most of them cannot remember a time when life was any different. The vast indifference of Americans to events outside their own country makes them unaware of how truly different their country is from the rest of the industrialized world with respect to violence and urban decay. When I lived in Europe, I constantly noticed that even the seediest western European city is far less dangerous than the inner zone of almost any American city. I found it particularly strange to be warned by American acquaintances about the risk of terrorist bombs in Europe, when in fact it was American cities I truly feared. More sophisticated Americans—the ones who realize that their country has problems—tell me that American urban violence does not distinguish the United States from other Western societies, but rather is the wave of the future for all industrial societies. They insist that as America has led the world in all things, so it will in this.

The condition of the inner-city poor, while the great tragedy of the United States, has not been without consider-able value for that country's political and economic élites.

In the 1990s it is easy for us to forget that full employment was once a serious goal of governments throughout the industrialized world. In the aftermath of the Great Depression and the alliance to defeat fascism, the balance of social forces in the Anglo-American world was very different than today: trade unions were strong and egalitarian assumptions were taken seriously. Moreover, relatively full employment in the postwar years heightened the bargaining power of labour. Conservatism was in retreat.

In today's Anglo-American world, by contrast, higher unemployment is the norm, trade unions are weak, and the bargaining power of labour has been reduced. In the United States the presence of a vast army of unemployed and underemployed people has had a huge effect on the social equation. Such people can be hired when they are needed and laid off when they are not.

The neoconservative onslaught succeeded partly because it offered a way to justify inequality. This played to the inclination of affluent whites to abandon the socially marginal. Conservatism was based on a negative view of human nature that saw people as naturally lazy and unruly, and needing to be hounded and spurred into productivity.

Conservatives have always been drawn to the stern virtues represented by the police and the military, believing that discipline must be instilled in the population and that, when necessary, an iron wall must be placed between decent society and a violent underclass. For conservatives, violence and crime are ready evidence that the human race is depraved. For them, the "counterproductive" behaviour of the marginalized supports their view that social programs can never succeed in overcoming poverty or redistributing income.

The conservatives have relied heavily on this perception of the inner-city poor to sell their critique of social programs. At the heart of this critique is the paradoxical idea that the poor need less money so that they will be motivated to work, while the rich need more money so they will be motivated to invest. According to conservatives, the social programs launched in the 1960s and 1970s have helped to establish a flourishing culture of dependency that has institutionalized permanent poverty and made its problems even more intractable. They argue that government programs to aid the poor encourage dependency and render participants less and less capable of self-help, self-discipline, and a successful entry into the work force.

Charles Murray, a Washington-based analyst, once made the further case that federal welfare programs were directly responsible for teen pregnancy among blacks. His reasoning was that teenagers were engaging in a rational economic activity by having babies, since it entitled them to federal income support, and that cancelling this support would reduce illegitimate births. (When I spoke with Murray at his home in Washington in 1985, he told me he had seriously considered advocating annual payments to non-pregnant teenage girls on their birthdays, as a way of discouraging pregnancy.)

Murray's thesis, more generally, was that in avoiding work, those on welfare were engaging in a rational economic activity, and that eliminating federal welfare programs would break the cycle of dependency and motivate most able-bodied recipients to find jobs. This would in turn—of course—reduce federal expenditures and ultimately federal taxes as well.

And just as conservatives were attacking the utility of welfare programs, they were also attacking the high marginal tax rates faced by well-to-do Americans. Supply-side economics, which was heavily touted during the early Reagan years, rests on the assumption that investment, which is the key determinant of economic growth, is profoundly influenced by tax rates. The argument goes that if taxes are too high, the rich don't invest, so to increase investment, government must lower the marginal tax rates. This spurs additional investment, which spurs economic activity, which spurs a high enough increase in tax payments that total government revenues do not fall. This theory has the charm of a perpetual motion machine: the rich pay lower taxes . . . the economy grows . . . and government does not even run a deficit. . . .

The idea that more for the poor is enervating and addictive, while more for the rich is energizing and productive, is what justified, in societal terms, the vast greed of the Reagan–Bush era. And what gave this analysis weight in the United States was not the brilliance of conservative political leaders but the nature of American society itself.

There is an unavoidable conclusion to be made: in marked contrast with every other advanced industrial country, the United States has failed to form itself into a single social and political community. What do I mean by this?

In an advanced democratic state, citizens enjoy at least some degree of broad moral equivalence; this is what makes them members of one community. I am not denying that major inequalities may well exist based on social class, religion, ethnicity, gender, and region. I am saying that in an advanced state, beyond the formalities of citizenship, political rights, and equality before the law, there are widely accepted mutual obligations, such as for social and educational programs, that bind society together. How far these obligations should extend is the subject of constant debate; some people want to increase them, some want the opposite. In any event, these obligations are always present—except in the United States, where the situation is qualitatively different.

(On this issue, Germany perhaps most resembles the United States. In Germany there are six million foreigners—"guest workers" and their families—who have almost no hope of becoming citizens. The Germans could change their constitution to allow these people to apply for citizenship, and are now heatedly debating whether they should.)

Whatever the Constitution and political system say, Americans do not actually see themselves as a single society within which people are obligated to each other. When blacks and Hispanics rioted in south-central Los Angeles during the spring of 1992, affluent white Americans saw them not as "fellow Americans" but as a problem. In his celebrated analysis of the United States, Alexis de Tocqueville was eerily prescient about the future relationship between blacks and whites in America: "The danger of conflict between the white and the black inhabitants perpetually haunts the imagination of Americans, like a painful dream."[15]

There are many reasons why the United States has failed to develop "social democracy" to the same extent as other advanced industrialized countries. Of enormous importance has been the cult of individualism. Louis Hartz, the great American historian, made the case that the original thirteen colonies were formed out of a highly concentrated fragment of European society and so reproduced only certain aspects of that society.[16] One result was that precapitalist values never took root to any significant degree in colonial America. This meant that the United States developed out of a group of colonies that constituted the most purely bourgeois society in the world, one in which individualism amounted to almost a national religion, with the Declaration of Independence and the Constitution as its scriptures.

Whether Hartz's model is accepted or not, there can be little doubt that the spectrum of legitimate politics has been much narrower in the United States than anywhere else in the industrialized world. In the United States the terms "left" and "right" have referred to a contest between "equality of opportunity," which stresses the need for everyone to have a chance in the competitive struggle, and "freedom of enterprise," which stresses the right of business to operate with minimal societal controls. Strikingly absent has been the kind of social democracy that has been important in every other industrialized western country.

The impact of racism and slavery on the American social contract must also be analyzed. It is well-known that racism can divide a society so that popular opposition to economic élites is transformed into interracial antagonism. According to Hartz and many others, the United States is the most fundamentally liberal of all societies. This is most true, of course, when black and Hispanic Americans are dropped from the equation. When they are included as a central rather than a peripheral fact of American life, it quickly becomes apparent that racial divisions have deeply affected American society and politics and arrested their development.

While the American Revolution opened the way for the consolidation of American democracy, it did not improve conditions for blacks to any appreciable extent. Indeed, slavery in the South, seen by many contemporary observers as waning in the late eighteenth century, experienced a boom after 1820, when the plantation economy was reaching its zenith. The Civil War destroyed formal slavery, of course; but after a brief period of radical reconstruction, white supremacists in the South were able to reestablish racism in both society and the legal system. The next major opening in American society came with the New Deal in the 1930s and lasted, with ups and downs, until Lyndon Johnson's Great Society in the 1960s. It was only in that decade, through the efforts of the civil rights movement, that the shackles of formal segregation were finally removed and that blacks in the South won the right to vote. Great Society programs also extended welfare state benefits to the poorest Americans and ensured more access to jobs for blacks through affirmative action programs.

THE COUNTERREVOLUTION

The gains that American blacks made in the 1960s, however limited, became part of the demonology of the new right in later years. Attacks on the Great Society became a staple of the conservative counterrevolution in the United States. This new movement began to gain ground in the 1970s and achieved its ascendancy with the election of Ronald Reagan in 1980. The advent of civil rights drove many white southerners to the Republicans. John F. Kennedy and Lyndon Johnson had won the South in 1960 and 1964; but after that, Republicans would always win the region, except in 1976 when Jimmy Carter, a Georgian, was able to reconstitute the old Democratic Party voting alliance between the South and the liberal Northeast.

In 1992 another southern Democrat, Bill Clinton, was able to break down the gates of the Republicans' southern bastion. To win southern votes, both Carter and Clinton had to make it clear that their views differed from those of northern liberals. Carter's born-again religious faith was reassuring to southerners, though it made northern liberals uneasy, just as Clinton's enthusiastic support for the death penalty appealed to the voters of his region, while troubling many outside it.

Many affluent whites, and many white ethnic working-class Americans, entered the Republican fold out of discomfort with 1960s-style radicalism. (The latter were the "Reagan Democrats." George Bush lost that constituency in 1992.)

The conservatism that took shape in the 1970s was complex, multilayered, and sometimes self-contradictory. It contained elements of both libertarianism and authoritarianism; it represented born-again fundamentalists and neoconservative intellectuals. Despite its lack of cohesion, it knew where its centre of gravity lay—in the rejection of the consensus that had dominated American politics since the New Deal. It asserted that the American system and way of life were fundamentally healthy and rejected the radical movements—black, antiwar, feminist, and so on—that had been so critical of it. It also insisted that the market rather than the state should set economic goals. Except for a few mavericks, conservatives rejected the idea of an industrial strategy and were also committed to halting the expansion of the welfare state—if they couldn't roll it back or starve it to death by fiscal means. Halting the expansion of social spending was, of course, intimately linked to the real heart of neoconservatism—the demands by corporations and affluent individuals for lower taxes.

John Kenneth Galbraith points out that affluent Americans—the contented who form the majority of the electorate, although not of the population—have a clear tendency to prefer "short-run public inaction, even if held to be alarming as to consequence ... to protective long-run action. The reason is readily evident. The long run may not arrive; that is the frequent and comfortable belief. More decisively important, the cost of today's action falls or could fall on the favored community; taxes could be increased."[17]

This mind-set that Galbraith describes so well has done a great deal to block increases in public expenditures for education and infrastructure, much needed though these have been.

The stagflation—that is, high inflation and high unemployment—that followed the world oil shock of 1973–74 undermined faith in Keynesian economic policies. Conservatives, principally the Friedmanite monetarists, challenged the theory that fiscal and monetary policies should focus on smoothing out the economic cycle. (Conservatives were divided in their economic thinking: monetarists believed in holding down expansion of the money supply so as to foster non-inflationary growth; supply-siders wanted to increase private sector investment by cutting taxes for the affluent.)

The attack on liberalism went well beyond economics. Law and order had become a white-hot issue. With the resumption of capital punishment in 1977 (after a decade with no executions), conservatism bared its teeth. Wars on drugs replaced wars on poverty. The reformism of the 1960s had groped, in its limited way, towards a new inclusiveness in American life; the new conservatives reasserted the politics of exclusion.

Capital punishment was both the symbol and the substance of the new exclusionism. It is not a coincidence that extreme right-wing movements always favour the death penalty. Nor is it a coincidence that among the advanced industrial countries, only the United States has reinstated the death penalty. Capital punishment is not about deterrence, nor is it about the cost of keeping murderers alive at the taxpayers' expense, although both of these arguments have been used. There is no evidence that the death penalty is more of a deterrent than life in prison. Furthermore, because the legal wrangling in capital cases is so expensive, it costs American taxpayers more to execute a criminal that it does to jail that criminal for life. The real reasons behind capital punishment are revenge and retribution ... and exclusion. The death penalty is the ultimate means of asserting that some people do not belong in society.

Between 1977 and 1989, 120 people were executed in the United States; 71 of them were white or Hispanic, 49 were black. Although the proportion of blacks executed in the United States after 1977 was not as high as it had been in the years 1930 to 1967, when more than half of those executed were black, it was still far higher than the black proportion of the population. (In 1986, 45.3 per cent of those in jail in the United States were black, 39.6 per cent were white, and 15.1 per cent were Hispanic or "other.")[18]

"Neoliberalism"?

The ideology born of a divided society occupied a highly strategic position in American life. It shaped the approach the United States took to the onset of the new global age.

In the last chapter, we explored the role of neoconservatism in breaking down nation-state barriers to the global operations of capital. Here our purpose is to look at the way in which a market-centred philosophy has affected the ability of the United States to cope with the global challenge. We need to further explore this ideology to understand that neoconservatism has not been an affair exclusively of the right. Indeed, its impact has come precisely as a consequence of its character, already noted, as a hybrid of liberalism and conservatism.

At the heart of neoconservatism is a call for the preservation or reassertion of classical liberal values—individualism, free enterprise, free markets, the limited state. The patron saint of neoconservatives is Adam Smith, the great eighteenth-century philosopher. The neoconservatives have always regarded Smith as an inspiration; even so, it needs to be pointed out that he made very different assertions than his modern-day disciples. Smith was an enemy of the aristocracy and of the type of mercantilism that is dominated by commercial capitalists (the ancestors of our modern bankers). His heroes were the nascent industrial capitalists. The present-day neo-conservatives have got it the other way around—they have been the voice of the bankers, and the short-term investors, and the coupon-clippers, and the *rentiers*; they work against the long-term capital needs, and the social investment needs, of the industrialists. They quote Adam Smith on behalf of those whom Smith himself would surely have considered the enemy.

Nevertheless, neoconservatism defends values that are unmistakably liberal. We can distinguish between that which is liberal and that which is conservative in the following way: conservatism is rooted in tradition, original sin, an organic conception of society, and a belief in hierarchy; liberalism is rooted in natural law, rationalism, individualism, and the idea of progress. In this sense, neoconservatism is clearly a variant of liberalism that accepts the premises of the modern world.

Much of the economic and political theory of the neo-conservatives comes from Friedrich von Hayek and Milton Friedman; what can be regarded as neoconservatism proper has a narrower focus, at least in the United States. Norman Podhoretz, editor of *Commentary,* is one of a number of New York intellectuals who shifted from radicalism in the 1950s and 1960s to neoconservatism. He towed his magazine with him as he moved across the spectrum. For Podhoretz and other thinkers like Daniel Bell and Seymour Martin Lipset—whose mentor was Irving Kristol (never a radical)—the goals were to affirm Americanism and to rebuff the new left's assault on American values. These people, who specialized in brilliant polemical attacks on the left, on socialism and Marxism, and on the New Deal and Kennedy–Johnson liberalism, gave American conservatism a literary firepower it had never had before. In the overall spectrum, neoconservatives were relatively moderate: while they believed in market economics, they also accepted a limited welfare state.

Today the newer American right—the "Paleocons"—regards this form of neoconservatism as nothing more than a variant of liberalism. Patrick Buchanan, an arch-Paleocon, deeply resented the influence of the neoconservatives and was determined to wrench their power away, as he made plain when he wrote, "Before true conservatives can ever take back the country, they are first going to have to take back their movement."[19]

In any discussion of neoconservatism, we cannot ignore mainstream American conservatism, which has been quite faithfully represented by William F. Buckley Jr.'s *National Review*. Buckley, who helped to rebuild conservatism after it touched its low point in the early 1950s, has steered a careful course between authoritarian and libertarian values. The critical anchor for his world view is, or was, the Cold War and anti-communism; he does not at all support the isolationism of the old right. Buckley is much more of a genuine conservative, in the organic sense, than the New York neoconservative intellectuals. As a result, his acceptance of the virtues of democracy tends to be conditional, and he hesitates in thoroughly embracing an antiracist position. Buckley has not always succeeded in balancing authoritarian tendencies with libertarian ones. (The tension between these two wings has been growing for some time, most notably on issues like abortion.)

Besides the conservative centre as exemplified by Buckley, there is also the new religious right—the Moral Majority, the evangelicals, and the born-agains. These groups have little in common with the neoconservatives.

Within the broad swath of conservatism, the neoconservative economists and intellectuals (and their British counterparts) have been the indispensable evangelists for international capitalism. They have committed themselves to extending the principles of American domestic economics to the whole world. Their program is basically this: free trade and free capital flow, without government interference. But it would be a mistake to conclude, from their enthusiasm for globalization, that they are genuine internationalists. The cultural and societal norms of the neoconservatives remain narrowly Anglo-American; they are actually missionaries on behalf of a particular civilization. And they believe that by pressuring other countries to play the game by neoconservative rules, the Anglo-American world will remain strategically dominant, its values prevailing. Certainly they have tried to deny to other nations the right to utilize state intervention. The purpose of this, of course, is to protect their world from threats by would-be economic rivals. (It is already too late for this strategy to be effective as far as Japan and western Europe are concerned.)

The neoconservatives did not invent the new global age; they have, however, been the prophets of a very particular approach to it. Paradoxically, they have achieved their influence because their countries are in decline relative to Europe and Japan. In fact, the cornerstone of their strategy—which is competitiveness through cost-cutting—only makes sense for nations in decline, and only as a response to "big spender" liberalism and social democracy. In other words, the doctrine preached by neoconservatives is merely the Anglo-Americans' defensive-aggressive response to their own decline.

The goal of neoconservatives has been to restore Anglo-American supremacy. Their means for accomplishing this has been to break the social contract in both Britain and the United States. The result has been a radical transformation in the Anglo-American world. Under Thatcher and Reagan, this world resembled a supernova—the grand explosion was a sign not of new greatness but of self-consumption.

The ultimate irony of American neoconservatism was that by concentrating its forces against domestic radicalism and the Soviet Union, it was seriously weakening the United States for the approaching economic battles with Japan and Europe. At a critical juncture between one technological age and another, American policies were pointing in the wrong direction.

Conservatives have a very particular view of what the state's economic role should be. In the late 1970s they rejected the idea of an industrial policy and lobbied forcefully for the expansion of the military as an instrument of American global power. In effect, they promoted an intensification of the Cold War rather than an economic battle against Japan and Europe. Military spending increased at the end of the 1970s mainly because of the conservatives' insistence that America was confronted with a "window of vulnerability." Their assertion was that during this dangerous time, the United States would be militarily inferior to the Soviet Union, but that increased military spending could close the window by the mid-1980s.

In 1979 and 1980 I conducted television interviews with Senator John Tower (later rejected by Congress as George Bush's nominee for secretary of defense); Alexander Haig, former supreme commander of NATO and later secretary of state under Reagan; and Norman Podhoretz. All three shared the view that the Soviet Union posed an ever more serious military threat, one that had to be countered through a major expansion of American military spending.

At the same time, core cities, infrastructure, and educational systems were allowed to deteriorate dramatically. For all the widespread rhetoric about the importance of education, the authors of the conservative counterrevolution were bent on reducing federal contributions to it. This, even though they generally agreed that the technological literacy of America's work force would be of critical importance in the new global era.

The state of American education in the 1990s bears the marks of years of neglect: 20 per cent of eighteen-year-olds are functionally illiterate; 25 per cent of teenagers do not complete high school. In a 1991 study of six advanced educational systems, American students placed last in mathematics and second-last in science. The vast majority of American colleges and universities have had to offer remedial classes to first-year students.

A pervasive tax-avoidance strategy on the part of American corporations has contributed to this sorry result. Typically, corporations have shopped around from jurisdiction to jurisdiction, enticing local governments to offer them low-tax deals in return for investment and jobs. The result is that in the average jurisdiction, corporations account for only 16 per cent of the property tax base. (In 1957 the figure was 45 per cent.)

This has savaged the tax base of many local governments. In many industrial regions school boards are now desperately short of money. While students are the imediate losers, it is the American economy that is imperilled in the long term.

A study by the Hudson Institute entitled *Workforce 2000* has forecast a profound shift in the American job market by the year 2000. In 1985 American-born white males accounted for 47 per cent of the labour force, yet between now and 2000 only one new job in six will be filled by people from this group.[20] The other five will be filled by women, non-whites, and immigrants. At the same time, the technological revolution is going to mean that workers will have to be better educated than ever before. Americans have long tended to let the future take care of itself and are far from prepared to educate and train their new work force in such a way that these citizens can fulfil themselves and that the country can be competitive.

The American mainstream has turned its back on the idea of making the public education system the central institution for educating all social classes. It has also been forced to recognize that a crisis has developed. It is one thing, however, for Americans to acknowledge the obvious—that without a strategy for developing technological literacy, their country will not be able to hold its own against Europe and Japan. It is another thing entirely to act on the problem in a way that doesn't make it worse. One trendy approach has been the voucher system, under which parents are given education vouchers and permitted to "spend" them on schools of their choice. In theory, this creates a market system of education in which schools are forced to compete with each other. In practice, this system is a recipe for inequality, for still more flight from the poor by the affluent and well connected. In establishing this system, Americans are moving ever further from the Japanese and European models for education, which are based on universality, high standards, and a thorough and sophisticated grounding in basic knowledge.

AMERICAN SUPREMACY IN THE NEW GLOBAL AGE

So far, I have shown that inequality is the central fact of the contemporary United States and has done much to render American society permanently dysfunctional. The divisions it has fostered are imperilling America's ability to survive its intensifying economic struggle with Japan and Europe.

American decline takes the form of a vicious circle. To understand how it works, we must consider America's changing global position.

Now that the Soviet Union has disintegrated, no one disputes that the United States is the world's only remaining superpower. The question is, is its position stable? Or is it already being radically destabilized as a consequence of economic (as opposed to political) competition with Japan and Europe?

According to one influential analysis, the international economic order always requires the presence of a dominant global power—a "hegemon"—that will ensure openness in trade and capital flows, as well as guaranteeing that all countries play by the same rules. The idea is that the hegemonic power provides the world with stability and a necessary degree of centralization. The two most obvious examples of such authority being wielded are the Pax Britannica of 1815 to 1914 and the Pax Americana after 1945. Such global authority is, of course, relative; no state can enjoy a monopoly of power in the international system—only a world state could do that.

For a state to become globally dominant, it must accumulate much more power than its competitors. How much power is enough?

At the end of the Second World War the United States had enough: its economy produced half of the world's goods and services. Since then, however, its output as a proportion of the world's has steadily declined. After 1950, the American growth rate fell behind that of the other major industrialized countries, with the exception of the United Kingdom. Between 1950 and 1983 the United States grew at an annual rate of 3.25 per cent; but France grew at 4.24 per cent, Italy at 4.26, West Germany at 4.63, and Japan at 7.87.[21] By the mid-1980s the Americans had lost their economic supremacy; not only had the economic output of the EC countries surpassed that of the United States, but the EC was on its way to becoming a single market.

In 1990 the American GNP represented only twenty per cent of global economic output. That it has declined in relation to that of other countries is in itself important evidence of a changed American position in the world—GNP is, after all, the broadest measure of economic weight. But the case for American decline by no means ends there.

At the beginning of the postwar era, American superiority was pronounced in four other critical areas besides total GNP: technological prowess, manufacturing capacity, the availability of surplus capacity for export, and military capability. By the early 1990s the first three of these advantages had crumbled to a greater or lesser extent, and the United States was much more dependent than in the past on its military strength.

In the early postwar period the United States had vastly better technology and business organization than its competitors. It had now lost its lead in the deployment of high tech— largely to Japan, although in some fields to Europe. In critical manufacturing sectors such as automobiles and machinery, the Americans have fallen behind both the Japanese and the Germans. In the mid-1980s the American trade deficit mounted and Washington began to rely on foreign borrowing to finance much of its deficit. This quickly eroded the American global financial position so that, in 1986, the United States became a debtor nation for the first time since 1919. Japan had replaced it as the world's leading creditor nation.

There can be no doubt that the strength of the United States has eroded relative to Japan and Europe. However, this is far from saying that the United States has lost its position as the preeminent global power. While American authority has certainly declined in relative terms, it takes considerably more power to establish world dominance than it does to sustain it. Furthermore, for a challenger to overturn the existing world order— even when it is headed by a weakened power—is an immensely costly and risky business. Before considering the possibility that the United States is on its way to losing its supremacy, let us consider the role it has played in the global system.

Over the past two centuries Britain and the United States have played a crucial role in establishing stable geopolitical systems. These nations have used their power to set rules for the global order and then to enforce those rules—policing other nations, rewarding them for compliance or punishing them for non-compliance. This has done much to prevent anarchy and conflict, and benefited all nations in the system to some degree. In this sense a dominant nation provides "collective goods." An everyday example of a collective good is a road, which everyone can use. In an international system, collective goods can include peace, international organizations, and a set of rules for an open and non-discriminatory economic system. In providing these collective goods, the dominant nation may have to assume disproportionate costs; for example, to maintain a high level of military capability, it will certainly have to make long-term outlays that drain its resources.

Other countries are unlikely to spend so much on their military, and can devote their energies to more productive activities. In effect, they take advantage of the dominant power's willingness to provide stability. These "free riders" constitute a major problem for the preeminent nation: in setting up and sustaining the world order, it must establish an economic system that will contribute to its own eventual collapse. To maintain the system it must provide collective goods; but in providing those goods it assumes long-term costs that undermine it relative to other nations. As it weakens, so does the global order it created, so that the system itself eventually relapses into anarchy and conflict. War may be the final consequence, as new powers emerge to vie for world dominance.

As a consequence of this vicious circle, it is possible to see the hegemonic power as an embattled and ultimately doomed character in the global drama. Because the hegemon does more than simply wield power—in the international realm it presents benefits analogous to those provided to a nation-state by a central government—its demise can be a matter for grave concern.

We can also understand the history of the past three centuries as having involved three different supreme powers—the Netherlands in the mid-seventeenth century, Britain in the nineteenth and early twentieth centuries, and the United States after the Second World War. In each case, the era of imposed stability was preceded by approximately thirty years of war. In each case the dominant power used its authority to uphold a liberal international order. In each case the dominant power was finally brought down—at least in part—by the costs it assumed in providing collective goods for the international system. These costs turned out to be unsustainable.

What happens when an old world order collapses? In a word, instability. Charles P. Kindleberger, who has contributed much to the study of hegemonic powers, concluded that the world economy collapsed in the 1930s because the United States failed to take the place of Britain as the dominant global power, and to fill the key stabilizing role that position involves, which is, lender of last resort. He concluded that such regimes are vital to a stable international economic system: "For the world economy to be stabilized, there has to be a stabilizer— one stabilizer."[22]

I return to the issue that concerns us—the decline of American global dominance. The following factors are of overriding importance.

- The return to "normal." Over time, the other major industrial countries that had been devastated by the war were bound to recover so as to deal with the United States on less unequal terms.
- The problem of "imperial overstretch." The Cold War motivated the United States to undertake a long-term military effort of global proportions. This had to result in a weakening of America's competitive position.
- The problem of "free riders." In pursuing its complicated goal of rebuilding an American-centred global economy while holding the Soviet Union at bay, the United States granted special favours to critically important regions and countries such as western Europe and Japan.

In Europe, West Germany turned out to be a classic free rider—launched with American aid through the Marshall Plan for reasons that had to do with American global interests, and ultimately growing strong enough to threaten American predominance. In Europe, West Germany (now, of course, simply Germany) was the most important but far from the only example of this: there were French and Italian "miracles" as well. By 1960 both West Germany and France had passed Britain in GDP. It would take Italy until 1987 to achieve the same feat, thus leaving the British economy in fourth place in western Europe.

The Marshall Plan was not the only American factor in the European recovery. There was also the stimulative effect of American military spending in Europe and—of decisive importance—the large-scale injection of private capital in the form of direct investment by American corporations.

While American policies were crucial to Europe's recovery, so were other factors. The countries concerned had been formidable economic competitors in the past and had the capacity to be so again. Also, West Germany, France, and Italy were all able to establish economic models in which the state played a much more active role than in the American economy. Corporatism, which establishes a social partnership between capital and labour of a kind that is inconceivable in the United States, was central to postwar development in Europe.

While Europe was recovering from the war and developing its distinctive brand of capitalism, Japan launched an even more spectacular economic takeoff. By the mid-1980s Japan was the world's most successful capitalist economy: its most adept user of high technology as well as its largest supplier of foreign capital.

These developments in Europe and Japan have created challenges for the United States—challenges that have become much more critical since the demise of the Soviet Union.

AMERICAN DECLINE

The unmistakable signs of decline in America have been observed by analysts from across the political spectrum.

A few years ago the doctrine of "declinism," as it was called in the United States, was most commonly supported by liberals. It was often associated with Paul Kennedy's book *The Rise and Fall of the Great Powers*. [23] Today, however, conservatives as well as liberals make the case that America is in decline.

One of the most vivid—and powerful—conservative portraits of American decline was written by Edward N. Luttwak of the Center for Strategic and International Studies in Washington, D.C., and published in *Commentary* in March 1992. In that article Luttwak argues that the United States will become a Third World country in the first thirty years of the next century, that "all but a small minority of Americans will be impoverished soon enough, left to yearn hopelessly for the lost golden age of American prosperity."[24]

Luttwak bases his stark conclusions on the fact that since 1970, American productivity has grown more slowly than either Japan's or Germany's. Japan has already passed the United States in per capita national output, and Germany has virtually caught up. He projects that by the year 2000 Japan's per capita GNP will be twice that of the United States and that the leading European countries will have a fifty per cent edge. He also expects that by 2020 Japan will lead the United States five-to-one in productivity, and that the richest Europeans will be twice as productive as Americans. At that point, he asserts, the United States will be a Third World country relative to Japan and will no longer be a serious competitor of western Europe.

Luttwak argues that the United States is declining because Americans have failed to save and invest on anything like the scale of their main competitors. Between 1970 and 1989 Europeans saved almost twice as much as Americans, and the Japanese roughly two-and-a-half times as much. Ultimately this must result in immense transfers of ownership of

American industries to the Japanese and Europeans. He believes that American policymakers simply do not understand "geo-economics," which has to do with the decapitation and acquisition of firms by foreigners whose goal is to capture the most desirable and productive industries, and who utilize government subsidies to achieve this.

A similar point has been made by Kenneth Courtis, Deutsche Bank's chief economist in Tokyo. When he testified before the Joint Economic Committee of the U.S. Congress in May 1992, Courtis offered details of the "investment gap" between the United States and Japan, pointing out that Japan is now investing twenty per cent of its GDP in new plant and equipment, the United States only ten per cent. Based on this, he concluded that Japan would continue to extend its manufacturing superiority and that in the first decade of the next century, Japan's economy would pass that of the United States in absolute size.

Lester Thurow, a respected economist at MIT, has also studied the relationship between the United States and its two leading competitors. In his book *Head to Head* he analyzes the competing strategies of the three major economic powers and concludes that the twenty-first century belongs to "the House of Europe."[25] He believes that Japan's economic virtuosity will remain unequalled, but adds that Japan simply isn't big enough to establish itself as the world's most important economy. The European Community, for its part, has already established the world's largest single economy by completing its 1992 program.

One unmistakable indicator of American decline has been

the rise of European and Japanese multinationals. The United States is no longer the automatic home of most global corporations. Thurow summarizes the changes.[26]

- In 1970, the world's 100 largest corporations were based as follows: 64 in the United States, 26 in Europe, 8 in Japan. By 1988 the numbers were 42, 33, and 15.
- In 1970, the world's 50 largest banks were based as follows: 19 in North America, 16 in Europe, 11 in Japan. By 1988 the numbers were 5, 17, and 24.
- In 1990, none of the world's 20 largest banks were American, and 9 of the 10 largest service firms were Japanese.
- In the chemical industry, the three biggest firms are now German-based.

Twisted and intertwined among its social, political, and economic components, the American crisis is stubbornly intractable. It is extremely difficult to foresee circumstances in which the Gordian knot might be broken so that the United States could proceed effectively to confront its problems. The dominant ideology of the United States is poorly adapted to mobilizing the country for competition with Europe and Japan, and the very elements of the crisis tend to reinforce its hold on the country. Widening social divisions and a growing separation between the white majority and the black and Hispanic societies help to sustain the hold of the ruling ideas on affluent whites.

The notoriously faddish nature of American culture and American intellectual concerns reinforces the severity of the American crisis. The reason is that short-term trends and shifts of mood are constantly obscuring the implacable reality that the United States for several decades has been declining *vis-à-vis* Europe and Japan. All economies have cyclical ups and downs, which means that at times American growth exceeds Japanese or European growth; this has often led analysts to conclude either that the United States has succeeded in overcoming the problem of its decline or that the problem never really existed in the first place. Changes in political leadership have had the same effect. When Ronald Reagan was elected president in 1980, there was, to use the cliché phrase, the feeling that it was "morning in America." The election of Bill Clinton in 1992 unquestionably lifted the mood of Americans, giving them the sense that they could compete effectively against the Japanese and Europeans, who were at the time having stubborn problems of their own. What is obscured by the conclusions drawn from the workings of the economic cycle or specific political developments is the long-term historical tendency that we have been analyzing here—a tendency that to date shows no signs of being reversed.

When the American crisis is considered in its entirety, we cannot help but reflect on the nature of societal decline. The decay of a social order is a deceptive phenomenon. Evidence for decline is found mainly in the increasingly dysfunctional character of social relations, political decision-making, and economic performance. Most measures of the growing stresses within these systems are quantitative rather than qualitative, so that their significance is open to reasonable doubt. What these signposts indicate is necessarily a matter for much debate. The vital signs of the social system do not quickly become darkly negative as the process of decline advances. Over time, however, the quantitative does indeed become the qualitative. Moments of drama signal the progression of chronic stresses to the point where critical breakdowns occur.

All of this is perfectly evident when we consider the most recent case of the collapse of a vast social system. The case, of course, was that of the Soviet Union, and there is no doubt that the process of decline was extremely advanced before its true extent was perceived either by analysts in the West or by scholars, dissidents, and political leaders in the Soviet Union and eastern Europe.

It is not difficult, in hindsight, to find the causes of the communist states' disintegration. Their commitment to costly and unproductive heavy industry, their agricultural crisis, their price subsidies for bare necessities, and the excessive material and social advantages that their top bureaucrats awarded themselves—all of these were heavy burdens. What finally sank the system was that once the whole labour force had been mobilized, there was no longer an unlimited supply of cheap labour to be tapped.

After the early 1970s, the countries in the Soviet orbit could no longer count on a plentiful supply of resources priced far below world market levels. To put off the day of disequilibrium and social reckoning, regimes such as the ones in Hungary and Poland borrowed vast sums from Western lenders. On borrowed money and borrowed time, the system was able to eke out another decade. In the end, rising external debt charges, the unsustainable costs for maintaining the system, and the absence of productivity gains all guaranteed catastrophe. When Gorbachev's reforms removed the threat of military intervention to sustain the system, it collapsed everywhere with breathtaking speed.

In the years leading up to the dramas of 1989–91, very few analysts were predicting such stunning changes. Many of the stresses I mentioned above were regularly discussed as features of the Soviet Union's chronic malaise; but the advanced state of Soviet decline was understood almost nowhere.

I mention all this not to predict a similar outcome in the very different case of the United States, but to point out that the relationship between the quantitative and the qualitative is elusive. There is a very strong tendency among social analysts to anticipate variations on past events rather than vast new transformations. It is always tempting to believe that a given social system is inherently stable. This is especially true in analyses of the United States, which is not just a nation-state but the most powerful and materially successful society in history.

There are, however, cogent reasons for believing that the United States is not in basic equilibrium. In fact, it is more plausible that the stresses on the American system are creating a state of disequilibrium that is becoming more pronounced.

Growing disequilibrium in a society does not strip those who belong to that society of their traditional aspirations. In the United States the material and social aspirations of affluent white Americans remain intact. However, the general environment of their country has changed dramatically over the past several decades. This can be seen most clearly in the cities, which have mostly become *terra incognita* for the middle class who once lived in them. When I first visited New York City, as a teenager in the late 1950s, I stayed in a part of Manhattan near the George Washington Bridge where I would not dare go on foot today. The emptiness of downtown Buffalo contrasts oddly with the presence there of some of the finest examples of urban architecture anywhere, in the works of Frank Lloyd Wright. The demise of the great American cities has not destroyed middle-class America, which has fled to its fortress suburbs. It has, however, vastly changed the way Americans must conduct their lives.

One sign of that change, seemingly minor but nonetheless revealing, is the way Americans now visit their cities. For the most part, my white middle-class American acquaintances have erected mental barriers to help them cope with the physical barriers they encounter in their cities. There are certain places they simply never go. Their visits are carefully arranged to focus on those Disneyesque relics of the past that have survived the vicissitudes of American-style development and urban rot. In fact, many of the urban treasures that Americans cherish are actually dead historic neighbourhoods from which real life has long since vanished and, furthermore, these areas are often surrounded by immense tracts of urban blight. Historic Savannah, Georgia, and Charleston, South Carolina, fit this description. Washington, D.C., is a treasure house of national monuments, splendid boulevards, and superb museums. The other Washington, with its crumbling buildings, its drug wars, and its daily toll of murders, intrudes to within a few blocks of the White House. For those who find the realities of American cities much too bleak to ignore, a solution can be found in places like Williamsburg, Virginia, a re-created colonial settlement—a town which never was—that has no actual inhabitants and therefore no actual social problems.

But most of the time the white middle class stays close to its private realm—nesting, cocooning, renovating—and practises systematic denial about what is happening in America. This should not be surprising—this is after all what social decline is always like. People shut out the dissonance and go about their private lives, trying to keep intact what they have always been used to having.

It must have been much the same in the Roman Empire in the third and fourth centuries A.D. Having lived in Provence, with its rich endowment of Roman ruins, I have often pondered the process of decline. A civilization does not collapse in a day. Rome was not suddenly engulfed by outsiders; rather, as Roman social and economic arrangements and political authority slowly disintegrated, more and more of the empire became dysfunctional, large parts of it reverting to a primitive localism. Some of Rome's successes, including its technology, survived for centuries after the fall of Rome itself. The magnificent 2,000-year-old Pont du Gard near Avignon was part of a brilliantly engineered aqueduct that continued to work for hundreds of years after the empire collapsed.

As for the American neoconservatives who have played such a vital role in unleashing the new global age—and, unwittingly, in speeding up the American decline—I suspect that they have been transitional figures, mere messengers, and that they will not be around much longer in the altered world they helped to create. They did much to usher in a global age; their attempts at "restoration" have set off a revolution. It is often forgotten that the French Revolution, which is commonly perceived as having begun in 1789, was actually launched in 1787, from the right, in the *révolte nobiliaire*, which was the last bid by the aristocracy to hold on to power. The group ended up being consumed by the revolution it set in motion. A similar fate may await the neoconservatives.

Instead of being seen as the age of globalization, the new age should be seen as the age of multi-polar capitalism whose chief outcome is American decline. Its principal feature is not the rising power of multinational capitalism but the ascendancy of multiple centres of global power. Whatever their problems, Japan and Europe are rising stars and have the potential to overshadow the United States. Since the end of the Napoleonic Wars in 1815, despite the interregnum in our own century between 1914 and 1945 when hegemony passed from Britain to the United States, the global system has been dominated by the great English-speaking powers. What truly distinguishes the era which has begun is the crisis of that system of dominance and the prospect that it will pass from the scene.

CHAPTER THREE

A CANADIAN CHOICE

Canadians displayed national disarray when they went to the polls on October 26, 1992, to vote on the Charlottetown Accord. There is no simple way to account for the Yes side's clear failure in so many critical regions. The stock explanations—Quebec was protesting that the Accord did not sufficiently protect its identity, the West was loudly expressing its right to be heard—do not fully capture what happened. In every region, Canadians were rejecting their political leaders, protesting their economic condition, and expressing fury at the way that Canada's élites were trying to alter their lives without really consulting them. Canadians had been warned by key political figures in all three main federal parties, and by all of their provincial premiers, that if they did not vote Yes, they would face peril. They chose peril. Their decision reflected the dangerous incoherence to which the country had been reduced.

Any explanation of the Accord's resounding defeat must begin with an analysis of the Conservative government and the way it understands both Canada and the world.

The Conservatives have been a one-idea government since the day they took power in 1984. Their one idea is that in order to survive the pressures of global competition, Canada must become a member of a North American economic bloc. The prime minister and his colleagues persistently claimed that among Canadians, they alone understood the imperatives of the age. It was in this spirit that they embraced the Canada–U.S. Free Trade Agreement as the cornerstone of Canada's future. The Tories portrayed the FTA both as a bold venture in which Canadians could test themselves head-to-head with the world's best (read "Americans") and as a safe haven that would ensure Canadian access to the world's largest market during a time of rising protectionism.

Their entire proposition rested on falsehoods: the Americans are no longer the world's best, so forming a bloc with them is parochialism, not globalism; and the FTA has prevented Canada from adopting an industrial policy that would enable it to compete with the Americans. At the same time, the United States is free to hit successful Canadian industries with countervailing duties any time it wants.

In their pose as the champions of a brave new future, the Tories have pilloried their Liberal and NDP opponents as mastodons, as stragglers from the vanished age of Keynesianism and the welfare state. (In failing to rethink their own positions, Liberals and New Democrats have made this Conservative task all too easy.) Brian Mulroney has described the critics of free trade as "neo-reactionaries," "prophets of doom," "timorous, insecure and fretful," and, above all else, "apostles of the status quo."

Once in office, Mulroney showed that he was prepared to push an agenda that was starkly at odds with the inherited wisdom of his party, which since the time of John A. Macdonald had always resisted free trade with the United States. The Conservative Party fought successful election battles in favour of a separate Canadian economy in 1887, 1891, and 1911. In the great 1911 battle, Robert Borden declared that the central issue was "whether a spirit of Canadianism or continentalism shall prevail on the northern half of the continent." He defeated Sir Wilfrid Laurier's Liberals that year. Comprehensive free trade with the United States would not become an issue again until the 1980s.

In the postwar decades it was the Liberal Party, historically the party of continentalism, that worked to integrate Canada's economy with that of the United States. In the end, however, it was the Conservative Party, which by the early 1980s was dominated by neoconservatives, that led the decisive battle against Macdonald-style nationalism. By then it was easier to find Amway dealers in the Conservative Party than people who cared about the ideas of Canada's first prime minister. The election in November 1988 was a turning point for Canada: for the first time, Canadians had elected a majority government committed to free trade with the United States.

In 1984, when Mulroney first won power, it had been different. Any analysis of the Conservative Party in that year would have made it abundantly clear that the party leaders were eager for free trade. However, the Tories emphatically did not make it an issue during the election campaign. Indeed, Mulroney himself was on record as saying he was against a comprehensive free trade deal with the Americans. After all this, the 1988 election became a virtual referendum on the

FTA. In that election just over 52 per cent of the electorate voted for the Liberals and the NDP, who were both committed to scrapping the deal; only 43 per cent voted for the Conservatives. Given the Canadian electoral system, that 43 per cent was still able to carry the issue.

My own reaction to that Conservative victory was typical of many Canadians. I felt that Canada had made a basic choice that ran directly counter to the entire history of the country. For me, the day after the Mulroney government was reelected was one for taking stock. I could not help but feel that the old Canada, the one in which I had grown up, had ceased to exist.

My thoughts went back to George Grant's *Lament for a Nation: The Defeat of Canadian Nationalism*.[1] In the mid-1960s that book had given an entire generation of Canadian nationalists its voice. When I first read it, at the age of twenty-three, the subtitle had meant nothing to me. What I did hear in the book was a powerful evocation of Canadian values, with their roots in romantic Toryism and social democracy, that drew a clear distinction between the Canadian experience and the individualism and imperialism of the United States. In the aftermath of the 1988 election, Grant's mature wisdom took on a different hue. In the book, after all, he had declared that his purpose was to "mourn the end of Canada as a sovereign state," that he meant his words to be not "an indulgence in despair or cynicism [but] a celebration of passed good."

After the 1988 election, I wanted to reflect on the "passed good" of Canada before trying to think about the future again. For me, the Canada that was departing from the stage was inevitably the Canada of Sir John A. Macdonald. Although it was never the product of any coherent design, Macdonald's Canada made use of tariffs, railways, and immigration to bind the country's regions into an economic whole. As the decades passed, Canadians traded more and more with each other and migrated to other parts of the country, and all of the disparate regions became a nation.

After the Second World War, on top of this economic base, Canadians built a national system of social programs and of revenue transfers from the richer to the poorer regions. Admittedly, this Canada was far from complete as a sovereign state: it suffered from marked social inequalities; foreign ownership was extremely high; the country depended on outsiders for new technology and for many manufactured products, while selling raw materials to make ends meet; and at the centre of society was a not very enlightened social élite.

Yet despite these limitations, the country managed to achieve remarkable economic expansion and enviable social stability. In the twentieth century Canada doubled in population relative to the United States. In the thirty years preceding the free trade election of 1988, its economy consistently grew faster than that of the United States. Especially in comparison with the rust belt American states that border so much of Canada, we had done very well.

But as I thought about it, I realized that the most important aspect of Macdonald's Canada was not actually visible. It was the hope for a better future—a future which Canadians themselves would design—that gave our system the utopian dimension so vital to the health of any political entity.

With free trade we were truly moving away from Macdonald's vision and towards Mulroney's vision. In Mulroney's Canada the economic links between the regions would ultimately be no more important than those between Canadian and American regions. It would no longer make sense to think in terms of a national economy. In such an altered framework, Canadians would almost be forced to familiarize themselves with the American communities nearest them. Life on this side of the border would begin to blend in their direction.

As Canadians, we are the product of our history and the keepers of certain social values that distinguish us from Americans. The strength of those values was obvious in the passion of the 1988 election campaign. Canadians wanted to believe that their distinctive society could survive despite economic integration with the United States. In Macdonald's Canada a national economy and a distinctive society had reinforced each other; in Mulroney's Canada the country would no longer be one economic unit but rather a collection of regions integrated with the continent.

After the 1988 election my first reaction to free trade was, simply, numbness. Throughout our lives we are often forced to reshape our identities, sometimes profoundly, as political and social structures and conditions change. People in the modern industrialized world have all done this before and many are being forced to do it again now. For Canadians, the present shift is far from being the only one we have experienced. Indeed I could myself remember an earlier one.

When I was a child growing up in Toronto, the two great patriotic days of the year at my public school were Remembrance

Day and Victoria Day. Of the two, Remembrance Day, with its military ceremonies, its marching music, its muffled drums, and its communal moment of silence, was much the more stirring, and the more anguished.

What public schools teach children always reflects wider social attitudes. At public school I became aware of the British imperial tradition, outdated as it was, before I developed any patriotic feelings for Canada. From my teachers I absorbed a Kiplingesque version of British imperial values, complete with "the white man's burden," that is, the notion that Britain had undertaken a civilizing mission throughout the world. Certainly, I had the impression that the British Empire was still the greatest power in the world. For me, the United States merely meant the rebellious Thirteen Colonies. How was I to know that the United States was now a superpower while Britain had been in decline for decades?

My generation was the last to be taught in school that the American Revolution was a subversive rising against the legitimate power of the British Crown. Although such a notion was far beyond me at the time, my teachers clearly meant me to understand that constitutional monarchy was the true path to liberty and that republicanism was a fast path to despotism.

But the Canadians of my generation were changing rapidly during the 1950s. They were beginning to accept things not accepted before—that Britain no longer mattered much, that the United States was uncomfortably close and huge, and that Canada had a difficult time making basic choices for itself and, having made them, seeing them through. By the beginning of the 1960s, we had adjusted our identity to the point that we were ready to abandon "God Save the Queen" for "O Canada," and to drop the Red Ensign for the Maple Leaf. In today's climate of weakening national identity, I cannot help feeling that we were blind to the advantages of automatic British citizenship, which we waived with so little concern. Had we been able to retain it, any of us would now be able to live and work anywhere we liked in the European Community.

In the 1960s, though, we were adjusting to the realities of our own continent and learning just how vulnerable our future was as a consequence of American economic, political, and cultural power. English-Canadian nationalists in the 1960s and 1970s believed that we could regain control of our economy through a state-centred program to transfer foreign-owned companies to Canadian hands. Left-wing nationalists supported public ownership, while those in the centre supported Canadian private ownership. There was, however, wide agreement about the nature of the problem.

The consensus among nationalists was that Canada needed to industrialize in order to cast off its historic role as a supplier of primary products to American industry. According to the nationalists' agenda, Canada would have to own a much higher proportion of its productive enterprises, and undertake more research and development, and manufacture more end products for its own markets. Such a program would create more higher-paying, highly skilled jobs for Canadians as well as promote economic, political, and cultural independence from the United States. Such views were typical of nationalists everywhere in the other dependent countries of the world—the goal, always, was to produce more and import less.

What made Canadian nationalism unique was its setting. Despite its resource-dependent economy, Canada was a developed country with a high standard of living, a strong domestic banking sector, an advanced educational system, and an economic infrastructure comparable with those in other First World countries. Canadian nationalism was an oddity in that it was not right-wing and inward-looking, as is typical in other First World countries. Instead it was tolerant and liberal, and at least as concerned with resisting aggressively right-wing American nationalism as it was with promoting Canadian values. At the same time, Canadian nationalism, much like the Latin American kind, was preoccupied with American control and with finding a way to industrialize that would let it avoid the "staples trap."

The nationalists' critique of Canada's economic relationship with the United States had a major impact on both the New Democrats and the Liberals. The Trudeau Liberals began to take initiatives that were based on that critique. They established these entities.

- The Foreign Investment Review Agency (FIRA) to monitor foreign takeovers of Canadian firms.
- The Canada Development Corporation.
- Petro-Canada, the Crown-owned oil company.

They also changed the rules for magazines so that *Time*'s Canadian edition could no longer pose for tax purposes as a domestic publication. And in 1980 they launched the most controversial program of all—the National Energy Program

(NEP), which sought to ensure that half of the country's oil industry would be Canadian-owned by 1990.

It would be wholly inaccurate to conclude from all of this that nationalists dominated this country's economic policy-making in the Trudeau years. During the 1970s, especially after the oil shock of 1973–74, monetarism and neoconservatism began to attract followers. Against them, nationalism was never more than a countertrend.

In the 1980s Canadian economic nationalism faced a series of crises, first in the battles over the NEP, later with the election of the Mulroney Conservatives, and finally in the negotiating and implementing of the FTA. The struggle over the FTA pitted social classes against each other in a spectacular but highly unequal contest.

Support for free trade with the United States had been building from the mid-1970s among the élites who were critical to its ultimate success. There was, however, nothing spontaneous about it. Important lobby groups brought together key representatives of Canadian business, neoclassical economists, and conservative political strategists, all of them essential to the campaign for free trade. Well before the Mulroney government was elected in 1984, the Business Council on National Issues (BCNI), the country's top business lobby organization, and the C.D. Howe Institute, a highly respected pro-business think tank, had developed a critique of the Canadian economy that focused on the benefits of free trade with the United States. Endlessly reiterated was the need to cut costs and to achieve economies of scale by dismantling protective barriers to outside competition and by gaining assured access to the

American market. If Canada was to transcend the limitations of the branch plant economy, in which local production by foreign-owned firms had historically been encouraged by tariff barriers, then free trade had to be embraced.

While the notion that free trade was a good idea was gaining ground among key groups of decision-makers in Canada, the specific initiative that led to the FTA, as Linda McQuaig proves in *The Quick and the Dead*, was actually the brainchild of American business interests.[2]

The élites, in promoting the idea that free trade was the salvation for Canadians, were embracing a much broader world view—in fact, an American world view. For me, in all the vast outpouring of analysis and rhetoric during the free trade debate, two encounters stand out. At a dinner party I asked a Canadian neoclassical economist why he supported free trade, and he answered simply, "You want to be poor?" That was the nub of the business élite's argument—that free trade was the way to achieve prosperity, for them at least. A week after Mulroney won the free trade election I met this man again. He told me then, with no irony intended, that his life's dream was to live in California. Alas, he was stuck with Canada, albeit a Canada he was helping to remake, presumably along Californian lines.

Our country's élite was abandoning Canadian ways—and economic solutions that had been central to the Canadian experience—in favour of American ways at the very moment in history when the decline of the United States was becoming obvious.

In Canada the state had always been at the centre of economic life, partly for reasons of circumstance and partly as a consequence of a very distinct history and set of traditions. The physical realities (that we are an immense, cold country with a small population, and so on) as well as the economic ones (that we were a late-industrializing country whose manufacturers had to compete from the start against British and American firms) made state activism a practical necessity. Such activism is typical of industrial latecomers; Japan, Germany, and Sweden being obvious examples. In Canada the state played an especially active role in transportation, communications, and energy. Under the National Policy of John A. Macdonald, which dated from 1879, protective tariffs were put in place to encourage Canadian manufacturing and reduce our reliance on imports. This policy also promoted regional specialization, with the West as the main staples-producing region and central Canada as the industrial heartland.

For several generations the key élites in Canadian business were wedded to this nation-building strategy. The bankers, railway magnates, and large manufacturers, and the businesses closely tied to them, profited directly from tariff protection and state spending on transportation and communications. Yet there was more to their support than simple self-interest. In the half-century between 1880 and 1930 the Canadian business élite was strongly pro-British, in the sense that they regarded Britain as a more desirable political, cultural, and social model than the United States. Business and identity went hand in hand, as indeed they would again when Americans began to dominate the Canadian economy. As late as 1939, Canadian élites were still identifying with Britain, the proof of this being their solid support for the Canadian declaration of war against Germany, only a week after Britain's own declaration, at a time when the United States was unshakably neutral.

The war changed Canada. If you had to choose the point in time when Canada's allegiance shifted from Britain to the United States, it would likely be mid-August 1940, during the Battle of Britain, when William Lyon Mackenzie King motored from Ottawa to Ogdensburg, New York, for a meeting with Franklin D. Roosevelt. King's desire to enter into a military alliance with the United States at that moment was rational enough: Britain seemed to be losing the war. Yet his headlong haste strongly suggested that Canada was deserting a sinking ship. The morning after their meeting in FDR's railway car, King and the president appeared together to announce that their two countries had just established a joint defence board as well as a permanent military alliance. King had always stood up to Britain, jealously guarding Canadian independence in matters of imperial defence, so his eagerness to embrace an American alliance was dramatic evidence that an important historical break had taken place.

Under the firm direction of the federal government, Canada used the war to strengthen its capacity to act as an autonomous industrial power. A highly successful strategy that combined public with private planning vastly increased Canada's industrial capacity and made it, for the time being, less dependent on American capital. At the same time, however, Ottawa was forging strong new political ties with Washington. Close working relationships began to develop between Canadian and American government departments. This functional as opposed to national approach to resource allocations for wartime production encouraged the growth of networks linking officials in Ottawa with those in Washington.

By the mid-1920s the United States had already passed Britain to become Canada's main trading partner and largest source of capital. By the end of the Second World War the Americans had more influence in Canada than the British— politically, culturally, and militarily as well as economically. By the late 1940s Canada was truly developing a branch plant economy, with American investors dominating the manufac- turing and resource sectors. When Lester Pearson, the external affairs minister, sided with the United States against Britain during the Suez Crisis of 1956, the change in Canada's world outlook was complete.

By the time the branch plant economy was fully in place, the "Canadian" business community consisted to a consider- able degree of executives of American-owned companies. In this, the golden age of American economic power, it was not just the representatives of American business who acquired an American-centred world view: Canadian bankers, large man- ufacturers, and small businesspeople had accepted the idea that the American way of doing things was the best in the world. In this shifting of Canada's focus from Britain to the United States, there was one constant, which was dependency. At the same time, just as there had never been a fully devel- oped Canadian point of view regarding the relationship with Britain, there would not be one regarding America.

This Americanization of Canadian business turned out to be a critical factor in the great crisis of the 1980s, when the nationalists fought it out with the neoconservatives in the free trade debate. By that time the United States was not merely Canada's most important trading partner; it was also the source of the neoconservative ideology that Canada's leaders had accepted in full. For people like Brian Mulroney or Michael Wilson, the notion of loyalty to Canada or Canadian ways could have no meaning.

The leaders of the Conservative Party and the major business organizations in Canada accept without question the American way of doing things; they have never seriously considered European or Japanese alternatives. They often quote like-minded economists to support their conclusions, but since these people are constantly doing favours for each other, this hardly gives any of them intellectual respectability. Their relationships are simply not arm's length.

The neoclassical economists, to whom business and the Tories turn for advice, characteristically present their preferred models for how the economy should relate to the state, and how business should relate to labour, as if they were the product of exact and impartial science. The truth is very different: economists are notorious for hiding behind their models, for using them as tools for advancing their own political and social agendas.

In the modern industrial world there are a number of distinct models for how the marketplace should relate to the state. These models are distinguished from each other by matters that lie outside the realm of economics. At their heart are axioms that are unprovable but at the same time embody values and assumptions about societal relationships.

We have already examined the socio-economic model

that has evolved in both the United States and Britain and noted that it rejects the very idea of an industrial policy and of a corporatist working relationship involving business, labour, and the state. Among the major industrialized countries, the United States and Britain have always been the most market-centred in their economic policies. It is significant that between 1950 and the early 1980s, they also had the lowest rates of economic growth.

The continental Europeans and the Japanese have employed quite different economic models. One extremely important result of the Second World War was that it established a balance of social forces in western Europe in which labour had much more clout than ever before. In the formerly fascist countries, business emerged from the war with its reputation badly damaged as a consequence of its active support for Hitler and Mussolini. This was true in France as well, where much of the business community had collaborated with both the Vichy government and the Nazis. Economic and social policies in France, Italy, and West Germany reflected this changed social balance, and still do. In one way or another, all of these countries have adapted economic policies that call for much more state intervention than is found in Britain and the United States.

In continental Europe, business and government have been much less successful than the Anglo-Americans at breaking the power of labour and forcing down wages. Since wages have stayed relatively high, these countries have pursued competitiveness through capital investment and by developing techniques for shedding labour. The European model has emphasized productivity gains and the use of industrial policy. With the European Community embracing a single market—and eventual economic and monetary union—this model is being transferred from individual countries to the EC as a whole.

The European model is embodied in the Social Charter, which was adopted by eleven of the twelve EC countries in December 1990 as a way of establishing minimum standards for pay, working conditions, and hours of work. This charter—which was sharply opposed by Britain, the lone holdout—makes it clear how much the mainstream political parties in Europe, both Christian Democratic and Social Democratic, share the assumption that market freedom needs to be limited for the sake of achieving social equity.

Japan has also adopted a model that is very different from the Anglo-American one. It is based on very close collaboration between the state and the corporate sector. In the postwar decades, under the guiding hand of the Ministry of International Trade and Industry, the Japanese set their economic objectives stage by stage. In the 1950s these had to do with overcoming raw material shortages and establishing heavy industry. In the 1960s the focus was on breaking into the global car market. In the 1970s and 1980s Japan systematically pursued breakthroughs in high technology and emerged, as I have shown, as the world leader in the deployment of computer-assisted production techniques.

Japan's model is not like Europe's, the main difference being the much smaller role played by labour, but even more different from the Anglo-Americans'. Both Europe and Japan have developed economic strategies in which the state works hard to mobilize key social forces in support of long-term economic goals. In the post-Cold War world, capitalism is divided between those countries deploying state interventionist strategies and those relying much more on the market.

It is a mark of the utter parochialism of Canadian business and the Conservative Party that the Anglo-American model has been adopted in this country so uncritically. We should recognize this for the tragedy it is. Since European settlement began in the early seventeenth century, Canadians have lived through a succession of historical ages and have always adapted to their imperatives. It is noteworthy that in each historical period, Canada was economically and strategically associated with the particular power that dominated the Western world. In the seventeenth and eighteenth centuries, before the British conquest, Canada was part of France's empire. Significantly, Canada was ceded to Britain, through the Treaty of Paris in 1763, just as Britain was launching its first Industrial Revolution. In the nineteenth century Canada developed within the all-powerful British Empire. By the end of that century, with the rise of Germany and the United States, British hegemony began to be seriously challenged.

As Britain declined relative to its challengers, the British élites grew increasingly worried, and a significant body of opinion developed in favour of a strident neo-imperialism. The goal of this new movement was to reverse Britain's decline by moulding the far-flung empire into a cohesive economic and political system.

Many Canadians were caught up in the new imperialism. A significant number of English Canadians came out in favour of an imperial federation, in which there would be an imperial parliament sitting in London to which Canadians would elect members. To stave off economic challenges from Germany and the United States, a common tariff wall would be erected around the empire. Incredibly, Canada came close to agreeing to all this just as Britain was entering its century of decline. In retrospect, it is easy to see what a misguided and even tragic choice this would have been.

Of course, by rejecting an imperial federation, Canada shifted from the British to the American economic and strategic sphere. In the 1990s, as another world age begins, one in which the United States has entered a long decline, the Canadian governing élite is tightening our formal ties with the United States. The Mulroney government and the business community, with dangerous shortsightedness, are binding Canada more closely to the United States at precisely the historical moment when doing so makes no sense at all. In effect, they are making the mistake Canada avoided with Britain a century ago.

Nothing is more fatuous than to think it is preordained that Canada's economic relationship with the United States must overshadow all others. Before the mid-1920s, as I have noted, Canada did more trade with the British than with the Americans, and there was more British than American investment in Canada. Only seventy years ago, in an age when technology was much less advanced and distances mattered more than they do now, Canada's chief economic locus was a European, not a North American power.

Why, in an age of technology that makes distances matter

less, do we have to pursue an economic strategy far more parochial than that of our forebears? The answer is, we don't.

Canada now faces its most important choice in decades. Many would maintain that the choice was in fact made when the FTA came into effect in 1989. There is no doubt that if we continue to keep the agreement, sooner or later Canada's economy will be fully integrated with that of the United States. At some point in that process it will become extremely difficult for Canadians to summon the political will to reverse course. I do not believe, however, that we have yet reached that point.

Canadians should abrogate the FTA and implement an alternative economic policy. This will be far from simple to do, but if we don't do it, the cumulative costs of economic union with the United States will do us far more harm than the short-term pain of disengagement.

Economic union with the United States must inevitably mean social union. It is chimerical to believe that Canada can operate within a single North American market while maintaining social policies that differ hugely from those south of the border. Of course, variations do exist within the United States, and relatively minor variations could be sustained between Canadian provinces, or between some Canadian provinces and American states. Admittedly, economic union would not dictate absolute adherence to an American social system; however, it would narrow the range of effective choices to the point where eventually, to all intents and purposes, Canada would be operating within the logic of the American system.

What effect would all of this have on Canada?

First, we need to consider the possibility that Canadians

could significantly influence America's future. In this age of divisible sovereignty, it is not at all impossible for peoples to pool their sovereignty in order to arrive at more effective economic, social, and environmental policies. The Europeans have already established a process for this: major economic, foreign, social, and environmental policies are now being fashioned at the level of the European Community.

But this pooling of sovereignty has not been achieved without very considerable political controversy. As long as the questions the EC addressed appeared to be technical in nature, they were seen as mainly the concern of élites. However, when the Treaty on European Union was fashioned at Maastricht, the Netherlands, in December 1991, EC integration became a huge political issue for the peoples of Europe. Referendums on the treaty in Denmark (rejected), Ireland (widely approved), and France (narrowly approved) revealed a widespread fear that national sovereignty was being handed over to an impersonal technocracy, located in Brussels, over which Europe's citizens had no control. The anguished debate about Maastricht aside, I must point out that circumstances in the EC are very different from those in Canada.

In the EC, while Germany plays a central role, no single country is in a position to dominate the whole. On top of that, participation in the community has become a very public affair in every EC country—the media extensively cover the monthly sessions of the European Parliament (which is popularly elected), as well as the decisions of the Council of Ministers, the initiatives of the EC Commission, and the semi-annual meetings of heads of government in what is called the

European Council. So the general public throughout the EC is well aware that important decisions are taken in Brussels.

The contrast with the FTA could not be more stark. While Canadians are well aware that the FTA exists, few Americans are. In their country the FTA is rarely a topic of public discussion. There is no sense whatsoever among the American public or its decision-making élites that the United States has diminished its sovereignty in any way under the FTA.

Moreover, American and European attitudes towards the pooling of sovereignty are wildly different. All governments in the EC recognize that membership in the community places certain limits on national sovereignty, and that they now operate within a political culture in which they must take other EC partners into account. (This was even true of those who led the campaign in France against the Maastricht Treaty: these people always insisted that they were pro-Europe and had long supported the EC.)

In the United States, by way of contrast, the idea of pooling sovereignty with other countries is not even remotely part of the political culture. No American political leader, Democratic or Republican—and that certainly includes Bill Clinton—would countenance the idea of trading away political sovereignty. It has never been considered by the American élites, let alone by the general public. What is for Europeans an urgent question that is encountered daily, simply does not exist for Americans.

That this is the American attitude has major consequences for Canadians. It means that no realistic prospect exists that we will ever establish institutions with the United States (and perhaps other countries such as Mexico) that would deal with a range of common issues. The essence of such institutions, as the EC experience makes clear, is that they must have the final say in their areas of competence. Under the Treaty of Rome and the Single European Act, specific areas of competence have been assigned by member states to the EC. In these areas the EC Court of Justice, which sits in Luxembourg, is the highest court of appeal, overriding the high courts in the member countries. In other words, in these areas, the EC has acquired sovereignty. This will never happen in North America.

Some might suggest here that the FTA's dispute settlement mechanism is a supranational institution. In fact, this mechanism—which consists of a panel appointed by both countries to adjudicate trade disputes—falls so short of genuine supranationalism that it merely underlines my point. Under the FTA the trade laws of both the United States and Canada remain in place. No common code governing subsidies and other commercial aids has been agreed to. As a consequence the only power enjoyed by the dispute settlement panel is the power to determine whether, in a particular case, the trade law of either the United States or Canada has been fairly implemented. In the actual making of trade law, the FTA has no supranational component.

Furthermore, it is clear that the U.S. Congress has no intention of giving up its exclusive power to fashion American trade legislation. What this means is that if a common subsidy code is ever arranged between Canada and the United States—and the FTA specifically calls for one—it will only be because Canadians are willing to accept a code that is entirely satisfactory to the Americans. For Canada, economic integration with the United States means harmonization with the United States. It is a dangerous illusion to think that it can involve any process of mutual accommodation.

For all practical purposes, the principles of the present FTA are the only ones that are ever going to be enshrined in a Canada–U.S. trade deal. Canadians who believe that the FTA can be substantially renegotiated are deluding themselves. Given the Americans' commitment to a market-centred society, and their determination to pool sovereignty with no one, the only kind of comprehensive trade agreement that the United States will ever accept is one that maximizes the rights of capital and minimizes any social and environmental commitments.

All of this means that the United States can only enter comprehensive trade agreements with countries substantially weaker than itself. It can never consider agreements with equals, or potential equals, such as the Europeans or the Japanese. Moreover, in entering agreements with weaker countries, such as Canada, it will never consider enshrining social or environmental principles that would dilute the basic American commitment to free-market supremacy. It is simply fantasy for Canadians to hope that the United States will ever consider rewriting the FTA so that it includes either a meaningful social charter—one that commits both countries to a minimum wage, maximum hours, decent working conditions, equal rights for women and men, and an adequate health care program—or a mechanism to prevent business from shifting investment to jurisdictions with underdeveloped social regimes.

Because the Americans will never agree to limit "social

dumping" in a trade agreement, any trade deal with them will always result in relentless pressures on jurisdictions to reduce social and educational spending. That is, after all, the only way that the other partners will be able to prevent jobs from being moved to jurisdictions with still lower levels of public spending. The advantage under the FTA will always lie with those who are socially regressive.

Moreover, the United States will never agree to any free trade agreement that allows its partners to pursue their own industrial policies. The FTA requires Canada to reduce its scrutiny of American direct investment; it also grants American firms "national" treatment in Canada. Both these provisions prevent Canada from pursuing economic policies aimed at strengthening Canadian firms so that they can become national champions in key sectors. Such a strategy has been central to the economic success of many other countries.

Also constraining the formation of a Canadian industrial policy is the fact, already noted, that American trade laws remain fully intact as they relate to Canada. This means that any time it chooses, the United States can respond to a Canadian industrial initiative by slapping on a countervailing duty. Not only that, but American trade law defines trade "injuries" so broadly that countervailing duties can be applied almost any time Canada improves its competitive position. And since such duties are provided for in American law, there is nothing the dispute settlement panel can do about them. In effect, the FTA has opened Canada to virtually unregulated American investment and imports, while leaving the Americans free to protect themselves against Canada's exports.

The FTA is not and cannot be a trade agreement between equals. It will never lead to a supranational future in which Canada and the United States make decisions together at a continental level, but it will force Canadians to participate in the American socio-economic experience.

In the last chapter I looked at the future of the United States. It remains for me to do the same for Canada.

Today a social fault-line runs through North America. On one side of it is a nation caught in a downward spiral of limited government and widening social divisions. An affluent minority that controls the political process there has insulated itself from the rest of the population, which lacks the political power to change the system. The affluent are undertaxed, and are unwilling to invest the vast sums needed to rebuild the infrastructure, or to improve educational and social programs to a degree that would promote a single functioning society. In that nation a long-term process of negative social evolution, characterized by widening inequality, is continuing.

On the other side of this fault-line is a nation where social solidarity remains strong enough that an alternative dynamic prevails. There it can be said that "one society" survives, that political power is dispersed widely enough that social and economic policies are fashioned with a relatively wide range of social groups in mind. There, a relatively generous system of social programs is in place and can be expanded. Wages and salaries are comparatively high, and the trade union movement is fairly strong.

On this other side of the fault-line, policies aimed at dumping social programs, or at forcing workers to accept wage cuts and a loss of bargaining power, are not easily forced on the population. As a result, there is pressure for alternative policies aimed at increasing productivity and promoting the kind of economic restructuring that addresses the needs of all workers—professional as well as blue-collar and white-collar.

Most parts of Canada are still on this side of the fault-line. Our imperative is to keep them there, but because of the FTA, we are tilting in the wrong direction. The American experience makes it plain that once a two-society model is firmly entrenched, it is extremely difficult to return to one society. Prudence suggests that the American experiment is one which Canadians should at all costs avoid.

A QUESTION OF POLITICAL WILL

There is really no escaping the logic of the foregoing analysis. It leads to the conclusion that Canada should abrogate the FTA, and the sooner the better. But abrogation makes sense only if an alternative economic policy for Canada is possible. However, before we can consider what that alternative economic policy might be, we need to confront the problem of abrogating the FTA. How much would it cost Canadians politically and economically to end the free trade deal with the United States? Is it a realistic course for Canada?

No one should claim that this is a decision easily made. The case for abrogation has been presented, but to that case must be added an assessment of how great the turbulence of cancellation would actually be.

At the very centre of the predicament that now faces

Canadians is the question of political will. Most Canadians, as public opinion polls have repeatedly shown, do not think this country obtained a good deal in the FTA. It is quite possible to make a convincing case that we would be better off abrogating the FTA and adopting an alternative economic strategy. In principle, many of us—perhaps most of us—could be won to such a proposition. Yet there is an air of unreality about such discussions, and unless we explore why this is so, we will not be able to make progress on this extraordinarily important issue.

Although they do not normally think of it this way, many Canadians believe that we are unable to adopt a rational economic strategy, not because it would be too difficult to design, but because we would not be allowed to implement it. To put it bluntly, there is a widespread conviction that we would be punished by powerful global economic actors who are determined to make an example of any country that attempts to challenge their authority.

It is this conviction—this fear of the consequences of acting together in their own interest—that is the real barrier to Canadians' elaborating an alternative economic strategy. Immense pressure has been applied to convince Canadians that their only option is to live according to the rule book of globalization. As we have seen, globalization presents a false analysis of the world; nonetheless, it is a formidable agenda that powerful interests have raised as a means to reorder society to suit their purposes.

A decade ago Canadians still believed—indeed, took it for granted—that their national government had the power to make decisions about vital questions. Today that notion, which is so central to our existence as a democratic society, is disappearing. The FTA and NAFTA and the rest of the Conservative government's globalization agenda have undermined our tradition of political democracy so that we now accept something ominously different—which is, the necessity of being taken into trusteeship by multinational business. All of our governments, federal and provincial, of whatever political stripe, now act according to this imperative.

Cancellation of the FTA would involve a direct political confrontation between the Canadian and American governments. As Canada decided on abrogation and moved to carry out that decision, Canadians would be subjected to a hurricane of dire forecasts and even to deliberate efforts to destabilize their government and undermine its political will. There is no avoiding the fact that because the FTA has politicized Canadian–American trade, our trading relationship with the United States will remain highly politicized during the process of abrogation. Any government that has been elected with the mandate to end the FTA will have to make its case extremely clear to the Canadian public so as to maintain its support throughout the process. It will also be necessary for that government to make its case to the executive and legislative branches of the U.S. government and to a wider American public. The case to be made to both Canadians and Americans is this.

Canada wants to trade fairly with the United States but does not want to operate within an agreement that involves much more than trade—specifically, that seriously reduces Canada's ability to implement its own economic and industrial policies. The restrictions on Canadian sovereignty in the FTA are unacceptable and require that Canadians either move further in the direction of economic and political union with the United States or abrogate the FTA. Since no appetite exists in the United States for a pooling of sovereignty with Canada, and since there is little enthusiasm for such an arrangement in Canada, abrogation is the only option that will allow both countries to return to commercial relations which will not result in a relationship that neither country wants.

While such a case would not win the approval of American decision-makers, its logic could be made clear to them, along with our determination to restore a trade relationship that has always been extremely profitable to American corporations and to Americans in general.

While the Clinton administration will certainly not welcome Canada's abrogation of the FTA, it will see the matter differently than the Reagan and Bush administrations would have. The FTA was not the brainchild of the Democrats; indeed, as we have seen, the FTA is infused with the ideological assumptions of small-government conservatism. To a certain extent, the Clinton team is moving away from those assumptions and towards a posture of greater government intervention in the economy. That makes the FTA an anomalous leftover from an economic era that has now passed in the United States. However, just because Clinton is more of an economic activist than his predecessors does not mean that he would tolerate Canadian violations of the FTA. The irony is that Clinton could use the FTA to keep Canadians living in the economic age of Reagan and Bush, while deviating from that approach for the United States itself. Nothing would be more absurd than for Canadians to be stuck with economic assumptions that the Americans themselves have now discarded as a failure.

During the debate about abrogation, the Canadian government will have to endure not only overt political attacks from conservative opponents in Canada and from the American administration, but also an assault from North America's private sector. American corporations will warn that if free trade is ended, they will shift investment south of the border. (The irony is that the FTA has certainly inspired numerous American companies to shut production facilities in Canada and to supply their Canadian markets from plants in the United States.) Canadian companies, similarly, will also threaten to move south. (Again, the irony is that because of the FTA, many Canadian companies have already done this, while those remaining have repeatedly argued that if we want them to stay, Canadian taxation and social spending will have to be harmonized with American practices.) The private sector is perfectly prepared to undermine a government it opposes—such as the NDP government in Ontario—by carrying out a "capital strike" whereby investment is kept low and economic performance suffers.

All that a government can do to answer political and economic attempts to destabilize it is mobilize public support for its policies and be prepared to increase public investment to offset any politically motivated decline in private sector investment. There is no escaping the fact that reestablishing the primacy of political democracy—a critical reason for abrogating the FTA—will depend on strong public support for what is being done. If Canadians can unite around the goals of renewed democracy and effective economic sovereignty, it will be possible to abrogate the FTA and to make losers out of companies that undertake politically motivated capital strikes.

This is because, despite all that has been said by globalization advocates, capital is very far from being all-powerful. Indeed, it is much more the case that capital depends on a cooperative relationship with society and the state, than that society and the state depend on capital.

Because of its strategic position, business can appear to hold all the high cards in a contest for power within society. And it is perfectly true that if the rest of society does not organize around its own interests, business will easily succeed in setting the agenda. However, despite the gaudy illusion of our age that wealth is created in financial towers and executive suites by corporate lawyers, the truth is—as it always has been—that wealth is created by the labour and creativity of the vast majority of the population, without which capital is nothing.

The real issue in contemporary industrial societies is whether the majority can rise above its myriad regional, occupational, gender, and cultural differences to stand up to the more concentrated power of capital. When majorities have done so, they have been highly successful in setting alternative social and economic agendas that have served broad interests while still allowing business to be profitable.

The business interests that have had it all their own way for the past decade will do everything in their power to ensure that Canadians never learn this elementary lesson about the genuine sources of wealth and power.

Everywhere that it can in this new global age, the power of capital is testing itself against other social forces for control of the state. Wherever it can, capital will reduce states to pliant tools. The states that can genuinely be called "sovereign" will be those which can retain independent decision-making authority. Those will certainly include the United States, Japan, and the key member states of the European Community. Whether these states will include Canada is up to Canadians.

AN ALTERNATIVE ECONOMIC POLICY FOR CANADA

What, then, would be the alternative economic policy that would replace the FTA?

It should begin by recognizing the essentials, which our present policy does not. It should recognize that the goal of economic policy is to achieve a desired social order; it should not assume, as the neoconservatives have done, that our social order should be the servant of competitiveness. An alternative economic policy for Canada should begin then by affirming that Canada's goal is to build one society and to fight the present drift towards two.

A one-society strategy can only be arrived at by building a broad social consensus. Canadians must come together and seek out ways that their country can increase its productivity—ways that are suited to the realities of the new global age. Such an economic strategy would clearly have to involve two things: a lot of specializing in those sectors where Canadians enjoy a comparative advantage, and a continued high level of external trade.

Since trade has featured so strongly in debates about economic strategy over the past decade, let us address it at once.

It is reasonable to assume that abrogating the FTA will result in a period of tension between Canada and the United States; however, it will not disrupt the overwhelming bulk of Canada–U.S. trade, because most Canadian exports to the United States are not made in arm's length transactions. Rather, they involve American-owned corporations shipping home raw and semifabricated materials. Most such materials are used in American manufacturing or involve oil and natural gas supply. By far the most important fully manufactured products exported from Canada to the United States are assembled automobiles and auto parts produced by American-owned firms.

The Conservative government has tried to portray the Canadian–American trade relationship as a window on the twenty-first century; it is actually a rear-view mirror on the branch plant economy of the 1950s. This relationship is today, as it was then, an outgrowth of Canada's dependence on resource extraction and subsidiary manufacturing, in a setting dominated by American corporations. Brian Mulroney tried to fashion a world-class economy out of that dependence, and has avoided dealing head-on with the glaring institutional limitations of branch plant economics. (Considering that our prime minister, before he entered politics, managed a wholly owned Canadian subsidiary of an American corporation, we cannot expect otherwise.)

The Conservatives have fashioned their entire economic strategy around the central weakness in the Canadian economy. It would be far more intelligent to recognize the weakness for what it is, and move on to better things.

A Canadian trade policy that anticipates the future should start out by recognizing the vast bulk of Canadian–American trade for what it is—the product of a past era in our economic history. Naturally, it does not make sense for us to destabilize this trade. But we do not need a comprehensive trade agreement with the Americans in order to trade successfully with them. As long as the American firms that conduct most of the trade continue to find it profitable, they will sustain it. We can also count on them to lobby Washington as hard as necessary to prevent barriers from being placed in the path of this trade. Remember that most of our southbound exports go to supply the United States with energy and manufacturing inputs, as well as automotive products from American-owned plants. Very little of this trade has ever been politically sensitive south of the border, which is why American media accounts of American trade problems centre on Japan, the Asian Tigers, and Germany, but hardly ever mention Canada.

Canada's alternative trade strategy needs to be global in scope. It should not rest on comprehensive trade deals, although sectoral agreements make sense, as do contractual links that allow for regular trade negotiations. Our federal government should avail itself of the procedures of the General Agreement on Tariffs and Trade (GATT), seeking GATT rulings when it believes our exporters have been victimized by unfair practices. It should also participate in GATT's general trade rounds, recognizing, of course, that in an age of intensifying trade wars between regional economic blocs, such general negotiations are likely to meet with only limited success. Even so, we can further our interests through these negotiations.

The fact that trade tensions are rising among the major global blocs is a very good reason to avoid membership in any bloc. Obviously, the only trade bloc that Canada could join would be a North American one that is subject to all the drawbacks discussed earlier. In addition, as a junior partner in an American bloc, Canada would be affected by all of the trade disputes between the United States and the other blocs, while having very little power to influence their outcome. In other words, Canada would simply be a passenger in an American stagecoach. Things would be different, however, if Canada steered clear of bloc memberships. Canadian negotiators would then be in a position to discuss Canadian trade problems and aspirations without being weighted down by all the negatives that result from an American link.

Living in the world outside the blocs, Canada will not be free of trade irritants, which at times will be major. However, as we have noted, inside the free trade regime with the United States, Canada is hardly free of irritants—some with other countries, some arising from the fact that pooled sovereignty is impossible with the Americans.

Once Canada has abrogated the FTA, developing a sound economic strategy for Canadians will be much more straightforward. We will be in a position to do something that seems impossible now—to fashion an economic strategy in which our trade policy serves our larger goals.

That strategy should strike a socially acceptable balance between economic restructuring, to promote specialization in those sectors where Canada has an advantage, and the maintaining of traditional sectors, which are important in providing jobs and in sustaining whole regions of the country.

An economic approach that stresses restructuring—the phasing out of declining sectors and the phasing in of emerging ones—will be critical to success. It will increase productivity, raise the overall standard of living, and strengthen Canada's position in global markets. Sectors that have been restructured to increase their productivity play a crucial role in any economy; not only do they generate a new level of wealth, but they also help to carry other, less productive sectors.

But not all sectors are going to become models of world-class efficiency. Traditional sectors exist in every industrialized country—sectors in which the advantages of local production remain compelling. Dairy production falls into this category. So do fishing, market gardening, and some types of light manufacturing (furniture, beer, construction materials, some textiles and clothing, and so on). In these sectors local production is very important in providing jobs and in supporting the urban or regional economic base.

All industrial countries are to some degree dual economies in which modern, technologically advanced sectors exist side by side with much less efficient traditional sectors. In some cases, powerful lobby groups representing the latter can act as a brake on economic development. The fact remains that such sectors can play a crucial role in the economic and social life of a country.

The market should not be allowed to establish the balance between the advanced and traditional sectors; such matters should instead be decided through a process of political debate. At present, discussions about this balance are generally shrouded in the mysticism of the market. Conservative ideologues like to maintain that a free market is the best possible tool for guiding economic restructuring. In this they are wrong—one way or another, government intervention affects every sector of the economy. There is no "clean float" among sectors that determines in some impartial "Adam Smithian" manner which activities should be emphasized and which de-emphasized. If we are frank in recognizing the importance of the state in determining such outcomes, we will be much closer to seeing the wisdom of open debate on the subject.

For such debates to matter, we need to change the way we make our economic decisions. We need a process of consultation and convergent decision-making that brings together business, labour, and government as well as other specific regional, environmental, and social groups. In Europe such a system is called corporatism. In Germany and Austria it is considered vital to economic decision-making. (The term "social market economy" is applied to the German approach.) While a market system and private enterprise are fundamental to corporatism, so is the addressing of social issues.

Corporatism allows all of the major elements in society to look at the future together and arrive at a common approach to it. It is more democractic than the *laissez-faire* alternative, because it assumes that economic decision-making involves major social groups other than entrepreneurs and investors. It is also more effective, because it can give all of those social groups a stake in economic restructuring.

The problem with economic restructuring is, of course, that it destroys as well as creates, that it produces losers as well as winners. In a *laissez-faire* system this problem is resolved in favour of the strong, who mask what they are doing to the weak by appealing to the impersonal dictates of the market. Those who are cast as losers, however, do not simply submit to their assigned fate. Instead they resist in those ways which are open to them. Two common ones are these: a strongly negative approach to technological innovation; and an approach to collective bargaining that focuses narrowly on wage increases and working conditions and rejects any wider considerations relating to the future of the industry. This mind-set often involves a destructively short-term attitude to public investment in social and educational programs and economic infrastructure, even though such investments are essential to future gains in productivity. It is entirely natural that people who see no stake for themselves in the economic future begin fending for themselves any way they can.

A corporatist approach does not eliminate such problems. It does make them more manageable, because they can be addressed more directly and resolved more democratically. This approach must rest on the principle that society as a whole should bear the costs of economic restructuring, so that the workers and communities affected by economic change are not left to fend for themselves. Especially critical is large-scale job retraining; but this must be done in the context of wider planning that sets overall goals for the economy. Unless such goals are established, retraining merely steers workers into low-paying service jobs.

Planning, however much neoconservatives hate the word, is needed if Canada is to achieve what other advanced industrial countries have achieved. Without it, Canada cannot hope to carve out specific areas of high-technology excellence so that it can hold on to portions of the global market and create skilled jobs at home. As I have shown, the Europeans have done exactly this with their aerospace industry, through the establishment of Airbus Industrie, a consortium that has won thirty per cent of the global market for civilian aircraft. Japan has had the same success in microelectronics. In both cases, forward planning that involved government and the private sector was critical to success. Only by freeing itself of the FTA will Canada be able to duplicate these achievements in appropriate sectors. If it doesn't take that step it will forgo the right to consider itself an advanced industrial country.

Success in high technology will require a carefully plotted strategy of launching national champions. To nurture such firms and help them to hold their own against their global competitors, Ottawa will have to adjust its policies—for example, by changing its antitrust laws. At present, however, to do so would be inconsistent with the national treatment accorded American firms under the FTA.

Besides encouraging its own multinationals, Canada must also establish a clear policy relating to foreign multinationals. We are living in the golden age of multinationals. It is vitally important that we find a way to influence their Canadian operations so that they reinforce rather than work against Canada's policies. Otherwise they will continue to be obstacles to the achieving of Canadian economic goals.

A multinational corporation acts to maximize its global profits and is prepared to alter its internal pricing arrangements, as well as its income in particular countries, to reduce its tax burden. Moreover, it tends to involve itself in research and development with other companies in the vicinity of its head office. The result is that an R & D centre is established which benefits the companies involved in it but harms companies in those countries where the multinational operates subsidiaries. In addition, a multinational often has a special working relationship with the government of its home country, and in that sense is an instrument of the economic policy of that country.

Canada has attracted a uniquely high level of foreign direct investment and so has been hurt by the multinationals' practices perhaps more than any other country. This has inhibited Canadian R & D. It is also the big reason why Canada has been locked into its traditional role as supplier of raw and semiprocessed materials. Machinery production and basic manufacturing are typically carried out elsewhere.

This is a very old problem with no easy solution. In beginning the search for one, our government must acknowledge that a problem exists—something the Mulroney government never did. After that, it must establish a policy which accepts that the relationship between Canada and the foreign-based multinationals must involve a trade-off. In return for supplying resources for the multinationals and buying their goods, Canadians have a right to demand jobs, and Canadian-based R & D, and reinvestment of the profits earned in this country, as well as more opportunities to produce goods. Methods for asserting this right have long been debated in Canada. These two are often put forward.

- The careful screening of foreign investment and takeovers to assess their impact on Canada.
- In specific industries, the establishing of performance commitments for multinationals. In return for access to the Canadian market, foreign firms would have to create jobs, produce goods, and engage in R & D.

This second method was applied when the 1965 Autopact with the United States was negotiated: Canada was guaranteed the right to produce a certain number of cars and auto parts.

For it to work, and for it to express a broad consensus, the new economic policy must also be a social policy. This means it will have to be based on egalitarian principles. This will mean rejecting the neoconservatives' proposition that there is a necessary connection between inequality and wealth creation.

All of this will mean turning away from the Thatcher–Reagan world view that has dominated economic practice for over a decade. At the heart of corporatism is the idea that if the major groups in a society feel they have a stake in the economic and social agenda, they are bound to work harder and produce more. On the whole, this is more convincing than the conservative idea that wealth creation is undertaken by a relative few, once they are sufficiently motivated, and that society as a whole then benefits from the "trickle down" that follows.

A strategy for achieving social solidarity will necessarily involve heavy investments in education, social programs, and infrastructure. Such investments will be essential to maximizing productivity in key sectors. And productivity will have to be maximized before workers can receive the wage gains they expect. Neoconservatism always had the effect of pushing workers' salaries down; corporatism addresses the aspirations of workers, not only for fairer pay but for greater control of their work environment.

The need for investment, much of it public, to create the conditions for social equity, and to restart the economy in a period of chronic recession, raises the question of what constitutes fair taxation. Neoconservative regimes always made it simpler for the affluent to avoid taxes—indeed, that was the basis of their political popularity. Both Reaganism and Thatcherism rested on a frank appeal to the affluent but powerful minority; American Republicans and British Conservatives both became masters at promoting tax avoidance for the well-off.

No alternative to neoconservatism will be possible without a victory for the political forces that favour a fair and progressive tax system. It is the skewed approach to taxation that has undercut necessary public investment in the English-speaking world. The absence of such investment has weakened the United States, Britain, and Canada in their economic battle with Europe and Japan. It has also forced them to adopt a socially divisive policy of wage and social program cuts to achieve international competitiveness.

Tax reform is also key to addressing the problem of the federal government's deficit. The deficit remains the overriding policy concern of neoconservatives—indeed, it is their fixation. Having presided over the explosion of the deficit, both in Canada and the United States, the neoconservatives are now using the issue to justify an ever-widening income gap between the rich and the poor. At the same time, they misrepresent the deficit issue when they fail to make a distinction between investments by government, which lead to increased economic output and therefore an expansion of the tax base, and the day-to-day expenditures of government departments. They would certainly never be guilty of such an absurd error when analyzing the investments of a private corporation. The reason they make it for government investments has to do with their faulty, ideologically based assumption that governments cannot engage in productive economic activity.

The question of government investment in productive economic activities aside, the solution to the deficit lies in establishing a progressive tax system in which corporations and affluent individuals actually pay their fair share. The key to this is not a miserly social policy but rather the elimination of the loopholes that allow the wealthy and the powerful to write off billions of dollars in income each year.

If we are ever to arrive at sound economic and social policies, we as Canadians will have to debate our tax system. This is bound to be difficult—the affluent will organize and spend a fortune to retain their unfair advantages—but there is no way to avoid it if we are to restore social solidarity and if Canada is to achieve a high-productivity, high-wage economy.

Finally, this: Canada must establish a new set of policies aimed at carving out a strong position in the emerging global economy. The apostles of globalization want us to believe that the industrial world is turning into a stateless one. The opposite is true—today's world is characterized more than anything else by a fierce struggle over which states will emerge as sovereign states in the new global economy. By "sovereign" I don't mean autarchic, or acting in isolation; rather, I am thinking in terms of the ability of states or economic blocs to retain sufficient leverage to establish their own economic and social agendas. In the new global age, some states will be better able than others.

Those most likely to retain this power will be Japan, the United States, and the European Community. Should Canada be another? And will it be?

In my opinion, the answer is yes to both questions. It is clear that in this decade Canadians, consciously or not, are going to determine their own fate. Until now, we have always rejected continental integration, and I believe we will again and will be stronger for it in the new age that has begun. And it is something we should do, not because supranational arrangements are bad by nature, but because shared sovereignty with the United States will never be possible.

THE CANADIAN QUESTION

This brings us, finally, to the "Canadian question," on which so much energy has been spent over the past thirty years.

In the six years since the Meech Lake Accord was first worked out between Ottawa and the provinces, Brian Mulroney presided over the slow unravelling of Canada. Having embraced globalization and stripped our federal government of its historic purpose—which is to develop the country's economy and social system—he then tried to find a constitutional agreement that would satisfy all of the provincial governments. He found one—and Canadians emphatically rejected it. For now we should stop trying to reform the constitution. It makes much more sense to prove that Canada can work than to seek yet another abstract deal to codify how it ought to work.

The constitutional debates brought many issues to public attention, such as aboriginal self-government, new deals for western and for Atlantic Canada, women's equality, senate reform; but only one issue—Quebec's place in the country—has the serious potential to fracture Canada. Putting aside constitutional reform is not going to make the Quebec question go away. It is likely, however, that at least for the time being, Quebec's place in Canada is better addressed in other ways than through direct constitutional negotiations. Canadians have debated constitutional reform for thirty years and have just rejected their governments' best constitutional offer. This is not the time to begin new talks.

The alternative approach to Quebec—and, indeed, to the other regions of Canada—is to elaborate economic and social programs of the kind discussed in this book and to let Quebeckers decide whether they want to be part of this renewal of the substance of Canada. Much more now than ever before, the decision about whether to remain in Canada rests with Quebeckers themselves. Those of us who fervently hope they will choose Canada can influence the result by trying to make our country the kind of country people would choose to embrace. This approach is non-divisive and aimed at all regions of Canada equally. In the end, whatever decision Quebec makes, Canadians should accept it.

Our experiment with the globalization doctrine has been a disaster. The neoconservatives' most reckless belief has been that they can divest Canada of its sense of direction and that somehow, the institutions of the state will simply grind on, as if suspended in midair. The absurd irony is that, having de-stabilized Canada to promote short-term gains for investors and business, they must now find a way to live with the result, which is a business climate that is less than favourable.

As the largest institution we have in common, the federal government has a critical role to play in helping all Canadians cope with the new global age. The state is not a vestigial remnant of a past age, as neoconservatives would have us believe; rather, it is a vital institution that can act as our "equal-izer," and we should regard it as such.

Canadians have so far developed few multinational cor-porations. With Ottawa's help, we can develop more. Histori-cally, we have imported technology and exported raw materials and semifabricated or assembled products. To develop beyond that, as we already have in some sectors, we are going to need active government. That is the real lesson of the new global age, whatever the supporters of the globalization myth would have us believe.

Historically, the federal government had always acted as the protector of Canadian ways. In many respects it was created to perform that specific role. There is some truth in the famous quip, by a Quebec opponent of Confederation in the

1860s, that Canada was "a railway in search of a country." In the first hundred years after Confederation, the federal government did what the private sector could not do on its own: finance and operate railways; develop public broadcasting and airlines; operate petrochemical firms; and provide a Canadian presence in the petroleum industry. Before the Mulroney Conservatives were elected, these were seen as legitimate tasks of the federal government; after they are voted out, learning to cope with the new global age will mean recovering our sense of Canada's history.

Instead of debating the provinces about jurisdiction, Ottawa should exercise its powers. It should establish an activist economic strategy such as the one outlined here, and work to develop this country's social welfare and education systems, as it has in the past.

Most Canadians, and that includes most Quebeckers, do not have a highly ideological view of the roles the federal and provincial governments should play. Rather, they respond to what works for them and for their communities. This is decidedly not the case with the regional élites, the most important being, of course, the Quebec nationalists. When Ottawa agrees to discuss the constitution as a solo issue, it always loses, because supporters of federalism are spread too wide and thin to defeat those élites in a focused debate.

It is entirely otherwise when Ottawa proposes specific policies. Ottawa never wins jurisdictional fights with the provinces about who is responsible for social or economic policy; but it can win practical fights, for example, to defend health care or to create new programs that Canadians will support.

In any abstract debate about jurisdiction Jacques Parizeau, the leader of the Parti Québécois, is very good at looking like the president of a future Republic of Quebec. He would look less presidential if he were seen to be blocking a federal proposal to increase funding for education so that it will accept children from the age of two (which is the model in France). Then he would be fighting against the real interest Quebeckers (and other Canadians) have in overcoming a severe child-care crisis that makes life especially difficult for working mothers.

The federal government will not be embraced by Canadians because it is intrinsically a good idea. It will be embraced by them because it has useful ideas and can do things that no other institution has the capacity to get done. Brian Mulroney's problem has been that he wants the federal government to survive even though he does not believe in an active role for it.

In the late eighteenth century, Canada emerged as that odd little slice of humanity which took those English-speaking North Americans who rejected the American Revolution and grouped them with those French-speaking North Americans who had missed the French Revolution. As a means of entering the world, this had its advantages and disadvantages. Those aside, what has emerged over the past two centuries is a disparate country that speaks two languages, contains many cultures, and holds to traditions and values far different from those of the United States. Although small in population, Canada is capable of coping with the world more effectively on its own than in a continental union or under the wing of the United States. For the sake of our children, for the sake of the contribution we can make to the wider world, it is this path we ought to take.

NOTES

CHAPTER ONE

1. Government of Canada, Report of the Royal Commission on the Economic Union and Development Prospects for Canada (Macdonald Commission), 1984.
2. Linda McQuaig, *The Quick and the Dead: Brian Mulroney, Big Business and the Seduction of Canada*, 2 ed., (Toronto: Penguin, 1992), Introduction.
3. Among the many analyses of Thatcherism, I would recommend Jessop et al., *Thatcherism: A Tale of Two Nations* (London: Polity Press, 1988). A brilliant discussion of the intellectual background to the Thatcher phenomenon is found in David Marquand, *The Unprincipled Society: New Demands and Old Politics* (London: Jonathan Cape, 1988). For the motivating forces behind Reaganism, see David Stockman, *The Triumph of Politics* (Philadephia: Coronet Books, 1986).

Chapter Two

1. *International Herald Tribune*, 6 Feb. 1992.
2. Stephen E. Ambrose, *Rise to Globalism* (New York: Penguin, 1985), p. 81.
3. Ambrose, *Rise to Globalism*, p. 86.
4. Irving Kristol, "The War of Ideology," *The National Interest*, Fall 1985, pp. 6–15.
5. Andrew Hacker, *Two Nations: Black and White, Separate, Hostile, Unequal* (New York: Scribners, 1992).
6. Hacker, *Two Nations*, p. 97.
7. Hacker, *Two Nations*, p. 97.
8. *IHT*, 6 March 1992.
9. Commission of the European Communities, Directorate-General Information, *Eur 12: The Europeans' Europe*, July–August 1987.
10. U.S. Department of Commerce, Bureau of the Census, *Statistical Abstract of the United States 1991*, p. 462.
11. *IHT,* 6 March 1992.
12. Arthur Schlesinger Jr., *The Disuniting of America* (Knoxville, TN: Whittle Communications, 1991).
13. U.S. Commerce Dept., *Statistical Abstract 1991*, p. 179; Statistics Canada 1991, *Canada Year Book 1992*, p. 251.
14. U.S. Commerce Dept., *Statistical Abstract 1991*, pp. 178, 179.
15. See Hacker, *Two Nations*, pp. 215, 216.
16. Louis Hartz, *The Founding of New Societies* (New York: Harcourt Brace Jovanovich, 1953).

17. John Kenneth Galbraith, *The Culture of Contentment* (Boston: Houghton Mifflin, 1992), p. 20.
18. U.S. Commerce Dept., *Statistical Abstract 1991*, pp. 193, 197.
19. *IHT*, 22 Nov. 1991.
20. Hudson Institute, *Workforce 2000*, 1987.
21. The Economist Publications Ltd., *Economic Statistics 1900–1983*, 1985, p. 127.
22. Charles P. Kindleberger, *The World in Depression, 1929–1939* (Berkeley: University of California Press, 1973), p. 304.
23. Paul Kennedy, *The Rise and Fall of the Great Powers,* (New York: Random House, 1987).
24. Edward N. Luttwak, "Is America on the Way Down? Yes," *Commentary*, March 1992, pp. 15–21.
25. Lester Thurow, *Head to Head: The Coming Economic Battle Among Japan, Europe, and America* (New York: Morrow, 1992).
26. Thurow, *Head to Head*, p. 30.

CHAPTER THREE

1. George Grant, *Lament for a Nation: The Defeat of Canadian Nationalism* (Toronto: McClelland & Stewart, 1965).
2. Linda McQuaig, *The Quick and the Dead: Brian Mulroney, Big Business and the Seduction of Canada*, 1 ed., (Toronto: Viking, 1991) pp. 128, 129.